Antony and Cleopatra

William Shakespeare

Akasha Publishing

Akasha Classic Series

Akasha Classics is dedicated to the re-publication of cherished works of World Literature. Many of these writings play a special role in recording the history of human kind, who we are and where we have been.

Akasha Publishing, LLC
877-745-7317
AkashaPublishing.Com

Antony and Cleopatra, by William Shakespeare

Library of Congress Control Number: 2009912214

ISBN-13: 978-1-60512-572-5   Hardcover
ISBN-13: 978-1-60512-610-4   Paperback

Shakespeare Titles

Title	Hardcover ISBN	Paperback ISBN
A Midsummer Night's Dream	978-1-60512-544-2	978-1-60512-582-4
All's Well That Ends Well	978-1-60512-545-9	978-1-60512-583-1
Antony and Cleopatra	978-1-60512-572-5	978-1-60512-610-4
As You Like It	978-1-60512-546-6	978-1-60512-584-8
Coriolanus	978-1-60512-573-2	978-1-60512-611-1
Cymbeline	978-1-60512-547-3	978-1-60512-585-5
Hamlet, Prince of Denmark	978-1-60512-574-9	978-1-60512-612-8
Julius Caesar	978-1-60512-575-6	978-1-60512-613-5
King Henry IV, Part 1	978-1-60512-562-6	978-1-60512-600-5
King Henry IV, Part 2	978-1-60512-563-3	978-1-60512-601-2
King Henry V	978-1-60512-564-0	978-1-60512-602-9
King Henry VI, Part 1	978-1-60512-565-7	978-1-60512-603-6
King Henry VI, Part 2	978-1-60512-566-4	978-1-60512-604-3
King Henry VI, Part 3	978-1-60512-567-1	978-1-60512-605-0
King Henry VIII	978-1-60512-568-8	978-1-60512-606-7
King John	978-1-60512-569-5	978-1-60512-607-4
King Lear	978-1-60512-576-3	978-1-60512-614-2
King Richard II	978-1-60512-570-1	978-1-60512-608-1
King Richard III	978-1-60512-571-8	978-1-60512-609-8
Loves Labours Lost	978-1-60512-548-0	978-1-60512-586-2
Macbeth	978-1-60512-577-0	978-1-60512-615-9
Measure for Measure	978-1-60512-549-7	978-1-60512-587-9
Much Ado About Nothing	978-1-60512-550-3	978-1-60512-588-6
Othello, the Moore of Venice	978-1-60512-578-7	978-1-60512-616-6
Pericles, Prince of Tyre	978-1-60512-551-0	978-1-60512-589-3
Romeo and Juliet	978-1-60512-579-4	978-1-60512-617-3
The Comedy of Errors	978-1-60512-552-7	978-1-60512-590-9
The Merchant of Venice	978-1-60512-553-4	978-1-60512-591-6
The Merry Wives of Windsor	978-1-60512-554-1	978-1-60512-592-3
The Sonnets and other Poems	978-1-60512-561-9	978-1-60512-599-2
The Taming of the Shrew	978-1-60512-555-8	978-1-60512-593-0
The Tempest	978-1-60512-556-5	978-1-60512-594-7
Timon of Athens	978-1-60512-580-0	978-1-60512-618-0
Titus Andronicus	978-1-60512-581-7	978-1-60512-619-7
Troilus and Cressida	978-1-60512-557-2	978-1-60512-595-4
Twelfth Night	978-1-60512-558-9	978-1-60512-596-1
Two Gentlemen of Verona	978-1-60512-559-6	978-1-60512-597-8
Winter's Tale	978-1-60512-560-2	978-1-60512-598-5

William Shakespeare
(baptised 26 April 1564 – died 23 April 1616)

William Shakespeare was an English poet and playwright, widely regarded as the greatest writer in the English language and the world's preeminent dramatist. He is often called England's national poet and the "Bard of Avon". His surviving works, including some collaborations, consist of 38 plays, 154 sonnets, two long narrative poems, and several other poems. His plays have been translated into every major living language and are performed more often than those of any other playwright.

Shakespeare was born and raised in Stratford-upon-Avon. At the age of 18, he married Anne Hathaway, who bore him three children: Susanna, and twins Hamnet and Judith. Between 1585 and 1592, he began a successful career in London as an actor, writer, and part owner of a playing company called the Lord Chamberlain's Men, later known as the King's Men. He appears to have retired to Stratford around 1613, where he died three years later. Few records of Shakespeare's private life survive, and there has been considerable speculation about such matters as his physical appearance, sexuality, religious beliefs, and whether the works attributed to him were written by others.

Shakespeare produced most of his known work between 1589 and 1613. His early plays were mainly comedies and histories, genres he raised to the peak of sophistication and artistry by the end of the sixteenth century. He then wrote mainly tragedies until about 1608, including Hamlet, King Lear, and Macbeth, considered some of the finest works in the English language. In his last phase, he wrote tragicomedies, also known as romances, and collaborated with other playwrights.

Antony and Cleopatra

by

William Shakespeare

Dramatis Personae

MARK ANTONY, OCTAVIUS CAESAR, LEPIDUS }
triumvirs.
SEXTUS POMPEIUS, DOMITIUS ENOBARBUS,
VENTIDIUS, EROS, SCARUS, DERCETAS,
DEMETRIUS, PHILO, friends to Antony.
MECAENAS, AGRIPPA, DOLABELLA, PROCULEIUS,
THYREUS, GALLUS, MENAS } friends to Caesar.
MENECRATES, VARRIUS } friends to Pompey.
TAURUS lieutenant-general to Caesar.
CANIDIUS lieutenant-general to Antony.
SILIUS an officer in Ventidius's army.
EUPHRONIUS an ambassador from Antony to Caesar.
ALEXAS, SELEUCUS, DIOMEDES } attendants on
Cleopatra.
A Soothsayer.
A Clown.
CLEOPATRA queen of Egypt.
OCTAVIA sister to Caesar and wife to Antony.
CHARMIAN, IRAS } attendants on Cleopatra.
Officers, Soldiers, Messengers, and other Attendants.

[*Scene: In several parts of the Roman empire.*]

Antony and Cleopatra

by

William Shakespeare

Act 4

Act 5

ACT I

SCENE I. Alexandria. A room in CLEOPATRA's palace.

Enter DEMETRIUS and PHILO

PHILO
Nay, but this dotage of our general's
O'erflows the measure: those his goodly eyes,
That o'er the files and musters of the war
Have glow'd like plated Mars, now bend, now turn,
The office and devotion of their view
Upon a tawny front: his captain's heart,
Which in the scuffles of great fights hath burst
The buckles on his breast, reneges all temper,
And is become the bellows and the fan
To cool a gipsy's lust.

Flourish. Enter ANTONY, CLEOPATRA, her Ladies, the
Train, with Eunuchs fanning her

Look, where they come:
Take but good note, and you shall see in him.
The triple pillar of the world transform'd
Into a strumpet's fool: behold and see.

CLEOPATRA
If it be love indeed, tell me how much.

MARK ANTONY
There's beggary in the love that can be reckon'd.

CLEOPATRA
I'll set a bourn how far to be beloved.

MARK ANTONY
Then must thou needs find out new heaven, new
earth.

Enter an Attendant

Attendant
News, my good lord, from Rome.

MARK ANTONY
Grates me: the sum.

CLEOPATRA
Nay, hear them, Antony:
Fulvia perchance is angry; or, who knows
If the scarce-bearded Caesar have not sent
His powerful mandate to you, 'Do this, or this;
Take in that kingdom, and enfranchise that;
Perform 't, or else we damn thee.'

MARK ANTONY
How, my love!

CLEOPATRA
Perchance! nay, and most like:
You must not stay here longer, your dismission
Is come from Caesar; therefore hear it, Antony.
Where's Fulvia's process? Caesar's I would say? both?
Call in the messengers. As I am Egypt's queen,
Thou blushest, Antony; and that blood of thine
Is Caesar's homager: else so thy cheek pays shame
When shrill-tongued Fulvia scolds. The messengers!

MARK ANTONY
Let Rome in Tiber melt, and the wide arch
Of the ranged empire fall! Here is my space.
Kingdoms are clay: our dungy earth alike
Feeds beast as man: the nobleness of life
Is to do thus; when such a mutual pair

Embracing

And such a twain can do't, in which I bind,
On pain of punishment, the world to weet
We stand up peerless.

CLEOPATRA
Excellent falsehood!
Why did he marry Fulvia, and not love her?
I'll seem the fool I am not; Antony
Will be himself.

MARK ANTONY
But stirr'd by Cleopatra.
Now, for the love of Love and her soft hours,
Let's not confound the time with conference harsh:
There's not a minute of our lives should stretch
Without some pleasure now. What sport tonight?

CLEOPATRA
Hear the ambassadors.

MARK ANTONY
Fie, wrangling queen!
Whom every thing becomes, to chide, to laugh,
To weep; whose every passion fully strives
To make itself, in thee, fair and admired!
No messenger, but thine; and all alone
To-night we'll wander through the streets and note
The qualities of people. Come, my queen;
Last night you did desire it: speak not to us.

Exeunt MARK ANTONY and CLEOPATRA with their
train

DEMETRIUS
Is Caesar with Antonius prized so slight?

PHILO
Sir, sometimes, when he is not Antony,
He comes too short of that great property

Which still should go with Antony.

DEMETRIUS
I am full sorry
That he approves the common liar, who
Thus speaks of him at Rome: but I will hope
Of better deeds to-morrow. Rest you happy!

Exeunt

SCENE II. The same. Another room.

Enter CHARMIAN, IRAS, ALEXAS, and a Soothsayer

CHARMIAN
Lord Alexas, sweet Alexas, most any thing Alexas,
almost most absolute Alexas, where's the soothsayer
that you praised so to the queen? O, that I knew
this husband, which, you say, must charge his horns
with garlands!

ALEXAS
Soothsayer!

Soothsayer
Your will?

CHARMIAN
Is this the man? Is't you, sir, that know things?

Soothsayer
In nature's infinite book of secrecy
A little I can read.

ALEXAS
Show him your hand.

Enter DOMITIUS ENOBARBUS

DOMITIUS ENOBARBUS
Bring in the banquet quickly; wine enough
Cleopatra's health to drink.

CHARMIAN
Good sir, give me good fortune.

Soothsayer
I make not, but foresee.

CHARMIAN
Pray, then, foresee me one.

Soothsayer
You shall be yet far fairer than you are.

CHARMIAN
He means in flesh.

IRAS
No, you shall paint when you are old.

CHARMIAN
Wrinkles forbid!

ALEXAS
Vex not his prescience; be attentive.

CHARMIAN
Hush!

Soothsayer
You shall be more beloving than beloved.

CHARMIAN
I had rather heat my liver with drinking.

ALEXAS
Nay, hear him.

CHARMIAN
Good now, some excellent fortune! Let me be married
to three kings in a forenoon, and widow them all:
let me have a child at fifty, to whom Herod of Jewry
may do homage: find me to marry me with Octavius
Caesar, and companion me with my mistress.

Soothsayer
You shall outlive the lady whom you serve.

CHARMIAN
O excellent! I love long life better than figs.

Soothsayer
You have seen and proved a fairer former fortune
Than that which is to approach.

CHARMIAN
Then belike my children shall have no names:
prithee, how many boys and wenches must I have?

Soothsayer
If every of your wishes had a womb.
And fertile every wish, a million.

CHARMIAN
Out, fool! I forgive thee for a witch.

ALEXAS
You think none but your sheets are privy to your
wishes.

CHARMIAN
Nay, come, tell Iras hers.

ALEXAS
We'll know all our fortunes.

DOMITIUS ENOBARBUS
Mine, and most of our fortunes, to-night, shall
be--drunk to bed.

IRAS
There's a palm presages chastity, if nothing else.

CHARMIAN
E'en as the o'erflowing Nilus presageth famine.

IRAS
Go, you wild bedfellow, you cannot soothsay.

CHARMIAN
Nay, if an oily palm be not a fruitful
prognostication, I cannot scratch mine ear. Prithee,
tell her but a worky-day fortune.

Soothsayer
Your fortunes are alike.

IRAS
But how, but how? give me particulars.

Soothsayer
I have said.

IRAS
Am I not an inch of fortune better than she?

CHARMIAN
Well, if you were but an inch of fortune better than
I, where would you choose it?

IRAS
Not in my husband's nose.

CHARMIAN
Our worser thoughts heavens mend! Alexas,--come,
his fortune, his fortune! O, let him marry a woman
that cannot go, sweet Isis, I beseech thee! and let
her die too, and give him a worse! and let worst
follow worse, till the worst of all follow him
laughing to his grave, fifty-fold a cuckold! Good
Isis, hear me this prayer, though thou deny me a
matter of more weight; good Isis, I beseech thee!

IRAS
Amen. Dear goddess, hear that prayer of the people!
for, as it is a heartbreaking to see a handsome man
loose-wived, so it is a deadly sorrow to behold a
foul knave uncuckolded: therefore, dear Isis, keep
decorum, and fortune him accordingly!

CHARMIAN
Amen.

ALEXAS
Lo, now, if it lay in their hands to make me a
cuckold, they would make themselves whores, but
they'ld do't!

DOMITIUS ENOBARBUS
Hush! here comes Antony.

CHARMIAN
Not he; the queen.

Enter CLEOPATRA

CLEOPATRA
Saw you my lord?

DOMITIUS ENOBARBUS
No, lady.

CLEOPATRA
Was he not here?

CHARMIAN
No, madam.

CLEOPATRA
He was disposed to mirth; but on the sudden
A Roman thought hath struck him. Enobarbus!

DOMITIUS ENOBARBUS
Madam?

CLEOPATRA
Seek him, and bring him hither.
Where's Alexas?

ALEXAS
Here, at your service. My lord approaches.

CLEOPATRA
We will not look upon him: go with us.

Exeunt

Enter MARK ANTONY with a Messenger and
Attendants

Messenger
Fulvia thy wife first came into the field.

MARK ANTONY
Against my brother Lucius?

Messenger
Ay:
But soon that war had end, and the time's state
Made friends of them, joining their force 'gainst
Caesar;
Whose better issue in the war, from Italy,
Upon the first encounter, drave them.

MARK ANTONY
Well, what worst?

Messenger
The nature of bad news infects the teller.

MARK ANTONY
When it concerns the fool or coward. On:
Things that are past are done with me. 'Tis thus:
Who tells me true, though in his tale lie death,
I hear him as he flatter'd.

Messenger
Labienus--
This is stiff news--hath, with his Parthian force,
Extended Asia from Euphrates;
His conquering banner shook from Syria
To Lydia and to Ionia; Whilst--

MARK ANTONY
Antony, thou wouldst say,--

Messenger
O, my lord!

MARK ANTONY
Speak to me home, mince not the general tongue:
Name Cleopatra as she is call'd in Rome;
Rail thou in Fulvia's phrase; and taunt my faults
With such full licence as both truth and malice
Have power to utter. O, then we bring forth weeds,
When our quick minds lie still; and our ills told us
Is as our earing. Fare thee well awhile.

Messenger
At your noble pleasure.

Exit

MARK ANTONY
From Sicyon, ho, the news! Speak there!

First Attendant
The man from Sicyon,--is there such an one?

Second Attendant
He stays upon your will.

MARK ANTONY
Let him appear.
These strong Egyptian fetters I must break,
Or lose myself in dotage.

Enter another Messenger

What are you?

Second Messenger
Fulvia thy wife is dead.

MARK ANTONY
Where died she?

Second Messenger
In Sicyon:
Her length of sickness, with what else more serious
Importeth thee to know, this bears.

Gives a letter

MARK ANTONY
Forbear me.

Exit Second Messenger

There's a great spirit gone! Thus did I desire it:
What our contempt doth often hurl from us,
We wish it ours again; the present pleasure,
By revolution lowering, does become
The opposite of itself: she's good, being gone;
The hand could pluck her back that shoved her on.
I must from this enchanting queen break off:
Ten thousand harms, more than the ills I know,
My idleness doth hatch. How now! Enobarbus!

Re-enter DOMITIUS ENOBARBUS

DOMITIUS ENOBARBUS
What's your pleasure, sir?

MARK ANTONY
I must with haste from hence.

DOMITIUS ENOBARBUS
Why, then, we kill all our women:
we see how mortal an unkindness is to them;
if they suffer our departure, death's the word.

MARK ANTONY
I must be gone.

DOMITIUS ENOBARBUS
Under a compelling occasion, let women die; it were
pity to cast them away for nothing; though, between
them and a great cause, they should be esteemed
nothing. Cleopatra, catching but the least noise of
this, dies instantly; I have seen her die twenty
times upon far poorer moment: I do think there is
mettle in death, which commits some loving act upon
her, she hath such a celerity in dying.

MARK ANTONY
She is cunning past man's thought.

Exit ALEXAS

DOMITIUS ENOBARBUS
Alack, sir, no; her passions are made of nothing but
the finest part of pure love: we cannot call her
winds and waters sighs and tears; they are greater
storms and tempests than almanacs can report: this
cannot be cunning in her; if it be, she makes a
shower of rain as well as Jove.

MARK ANTONY
Would I had never seen her.

DOMITIUS ENOBARBUS
O, sir, you had then left unseen a wonderful piece
of work; which not to have been blest withal would
have discredited your travel.

MARK ANTONY
Fulvia is dead.

DOMITIUS ENOBARBUS
Sir?

MARK ANTONY
Fulvia is dead.

DOMITIUS ENOBARBUS
Fulvia!

MARK ANTONY
Dead.

DOMITIUS ENOBARBUS
Why, sir, give the gods a thankful sacrifice. When
it pleaseth their deities to take the wife of a man
from him, it shows to man the tailors of the earth;
comforting therein, that when old robes are worn
out, there are members to make new. If there were
no more women but Fulvia, then had you indeed a
cut,
and the case to be lamented: this grief is crowned
with consolation; your old smock brings forth a new
petticoat: and indeed the tears live in an onion
that should water this sorrow.

MARK ANTONY
The business she hath broached in the state

Cannot endure my absence.

DOMITIUS ENOBARBUS
And the business you have broached here cannot be
without you; especially that of Cleopatra's, which
wholly depends on your abode.

MARK ANTONY
No more light answers. Let our officers
Have notice what we purpose. I shall break
The cause of our expedience to the queen,
And get her leave to part. For not alone
The death of Fulvia, with more urgent touches,
Do strongly speak to us; but the letters too
Of many our contriving friends in Rome
Petition us at home: Sextus Pompeius
Hath given the dare to Caesar, and commands
The empire of the sea: our slippery people,
Whose love is never link'd to the deserver
Till his deserts are past, begin to throw
Pompey the Great and all his dignities
Upon his son; who, high in name and power,
Higher than both in blood and life, stands up
For the main soldier: whose quality, going on,
The sides o' the world may danger: much is breeding,
Which, like the courser's hair, hath yet but life,
And not a serpent's poison. Say, our pleasure,
To such whose place is under us, requires
Our quick remove from hence.

DOMITIUS ENOBARBUS
I shall do't.

Exeunt

SCENE III. The same. Another room.

Enter CLEOPATRA, CHARMIAN, IRAS, and ALEXAS

CLEOPATRA
Where is he?

CHARMIAN
I did not see him since.

CLEOPATRA
See where he is, who's with him, what he does:
I did not send you: if you find him sad,
Say I am dancing; if in mirth, report
That I am sudden sick: quick, and return.

Exit ALEXAS

CHARMIAN
Madam, methinks, if you did love him dearly,
You do not hold the method to enforce
The like from him.

CLEOPATRA
What should I do, I do not?

CHARMIAN
In each thing give him way, cross him nothing.

CLEOPATRA
Thou teachest like a fool; the way to lose him.

CHARMIAN
Tempt him not so too far; I wish, forbear:
In time we hate that which we often fear.
But here comes Antony.

Enter MARK ANTONY

CLEOPATRA
I am sick and sullen.

MARK ANTONY
I am sorry to give breathing to my purpose,--

CLEOPATRA
Help me away, dear Charmian; I shall fall:
It cannot be thus long, the sides of nature
Will not sustain it.

MARK ANTONY
Now, my dearest queen,--

CLEOPATRA
Pray you, stand further from me.

MARK ANTONY
What's the matter?

CLEOPATRA
I know, by that same eye, there's some good news.
What says the married woman? You may go:
Would she had never given you leave to come!
Let her not say 'tis I that keep you here:
I have no power upon you; hers you are.

MARK ANTONY
The gods best know,--

CLEOPATRA
O, never was there queen
So mightily betray'd! yet at the first
I saw the treasons planted.

MARK ANTONY
Cleopatra,--

CLEOPATRA
Why should I think you can be mine and true,
Though you in swearing shake the throned gods,
Who have been false to Fulvia? Riotous madness,
To be entangled with those mouth-made vows,
Which break themselves in swearing!

MARK ANTONY
Most sweet queen,--

CLEOPATRA
Nay, pray you, seek no colour for your going,
But bid farewell, and go: when you sued staying,
Then was the time for words: no going then;
Eternity was in our lips and eyes,
Bliss in our brows' bent; none our parts so poor,
But was a race of heaven: they are so still,
Or thou, the greatest soldier of the world,
Art turn'd the greatest liar.

MARK ANTONY
How now, lady!

CLEOPATRA
I would I had thy inches; thou shouldst know
There were a heart in Egypt.

MARK ANTONY
Hear me, queen:
The strong necessity of time commands
Our services awhile; but my full heart
Remains in use with you. Our Italy
Shines o'er with civil swords: Sextus Pompeius
Makes his approaches to the port of Rome:
Equality of two domestic powers
Breed scrupulous faction: the hated, grown to
strength,
Are newly grown to love: the condemn'd Pompey,
Rich in his father's honour, creeps apace,

Into the hearts of such as have not thrived
Upon the present state, whose numbers threaten;
And quietness, grown sick of rest, would purge
By any desperate change: my more particular,
And that which most with you should safe my going,
Is Fulvia's death.

CLEOPATRA
Though age from folly could not give me freedom,
It does from childishness: can Fulvia die?

MARK ANTONY
She's dead, my queen:
Look here, and at thy sovereign leisure read
The garboils she awaked; at the last, best:
See when and where she died.

CLEOPATRA
O most false love!
Where be the sacred vials thou shouldst fill
With sorrowful water? Now I see, I see,
In Fulvia's death, how mine received shall be.

MARK ANTONY
Quarrel no more, but be prepared to know
The purposes I bear; which are, or cease,
As you shall give the advice. By the fire
That quickens Nilus' slime, I go from hence
Thy soldier, servant; making peace or war
As thou affect'st.

CLEOPATRA
Cut my lace, Charmian, come;
But let it be: I am quickly ill, and well,
So Antony loves.

MARK ANTONY
My precious queen, forbear;
And give true evidence to his love, which stands

An honourable trial.

CLEOPATRA
So Fulvia told me.
I prithee, turn aside and weep for her,
Then bid adieu to me, and say the tears
Belong to Egypt: good now, play one scene
Of excellent dissembling; and let it look
Life perfect honour.

MARK ANTONY
You'll heat my blood: no more.

CLEOPATRA
You can do better yet; but this is meetly.

MARK ANTONY
Now, by my sword,--

CLEOPATRA
And target. Still he mends;
But this is not the best. Look, prithee, Charmian,
How this Herculean Roman does become
The carriage of his chafe.

MARK ANTONY
I'll leave you, lady.

CLEOPATRA
Courteous lord, one word.
Sir, you and I must part, but that's not it:
Sir, you and I have loved, but there's not it;
That you know well: something it is I would,
O, my oblivion is a very Antony,
And I am all forgotten.

MARK ANTONY
But that your royalty
Holds idleness your subject, I should take you

For idleness itself.

CLEOPATRA
'Tis sweating labour
To bear such idleness so near the heart
As Cleopatra this. But, sir, forgive me;
Since my becomings kill me, when they do not
Eye well to you: your honour calls you hence;
Therefore be deaf to my unpitied folly.
And all the gods go with you! upon your sword
Sit laurel victory! and smooth success
Be strew'd before your feet!

MARK ANTONY
Let us go. Come;
Our separation so abides, and flies,
That thou, residing here, go'st yet with me,
And I, hence fleeting, here remain with thee. Away!

Exeunt

SCENE IV. Rome. OCTAVIUS CAESAR's house.

Enter OCTAVIUS CAESAR, reading a letter, LEPIDUS,
and their Train

OCTAVIUS CAESAR
You may see, Lepidus, and henceforth know,
It is not Caesar's natural vice to hate
Our great competitor: from Alexandria
This is the news: he fishes, drinks, and wastes
The lamps of night in revel; is not more man-like
Than Cleopatra; nor the queen of Ptolemy
More womanly than he; hardly gave audience, or
Vouchsafed to think he had partners: you shall find
there
A man who is the abstract of all faults
That all men follow.

LEPIDUS
I must not think there are
Evils enow to darken all his goodness:
His faults in him seem as the spots of heaven,
More fiery by night's blackness; hereditary,
Rather than purchased; what he cannot change,
Than what he chooses.

OCTAVIUS CAESAR
You are too indulgent. Let us grant, it is not
Amiss to tumble on the bed of Ptolemy;
To give a kingdom for a mirth; to sit
And keep the turn of tippling with a slave;
To reel the streets at noon, and stand the buffet
With knaves that smell of sweat: say this
becomes him,--
As his composure must be rare indeed
Whom these things cannot blemish,--yet must Antony
No way excuse his soils, when we do bear
So great weight in his lightness. If he fill'd

His vacancy with his voluptuousness,
Full surfeits, and the dryness of his bones,
Call on him for't: but to confound such time,
That drums him from his sport, and speaks as loud
As his own state and ours,--'tis to be chid
As we rate boys, who, being mature in knowledge,
Pawn their experience to their present pleasure,
And so rebel to judgment.

Enter a Messenger

LEPIDUS
Here's more news.

Messenger
Thy biddings have been done; and every hour,
Most noble Caesar, shalt thou have report
How 'tis abroad. Pompey is strong at sea;
And it appears he is beloved of those
That only have fear'd Caesar: to the ports
The discontents repair, and men's reports
Give him much wrong'd.

OCTAVIUS CAESAR
I should have known no less.
It hath been taught us from the primal state,
That he which is was wish'd until he were;
And the ebb'd man, ne'er loved till ne'er worth love,
Comes dear'd by being lack'd. This common body,
Like to a vagabond flag upon the stream,
Goes to and back, lackeying the varying tide,
To rot itself with motion.

Messenger
Caesar, I bring thee word,
Menecrates and Menas, famous pirates,
Make the sea serve them, which they ear and wound
With keels of every kind: many hot inroads
They make in Italy; the borders maritime

Lack blood to think on't, and flush youth revolt:
No vessel can peep forth, but 'tis as soon
Taken as seen; for Pompey's name strikes more
Than could his war resisted.

OCTAVIUS CAESAR
Antony,
Leave thy lascivious wassails. When thou once
Wast beaten from Modena, where thou slew'st
Hirtius and Pansa, consuls, at thy heel
Did famine follow; whom thou fought'st against,
Though daintily brought up, with patience more
Than savages could suffer: thou didst drink
The stale of horses, and the gilded puddle
Which beasts would cough at: thy palate then did
deign
The roughest berry on the rudest hedge;
Yea, like the stag, when snow the pasture sheets,
The barks of trees thou browsed'st; on the Alps
It is reported thou didst eat strange flesh,
Which some did die to look on: and all this--
It wounds thine honour that I speak it now--
Was borne so like a soldier, that thy cheek
So much as lank'd not.

LEPIDUS
'Tis pity of him.

OCTAVIUS CAESAR
Let his shames quickly
Drive him to Rome: 'tis time we twain
Did show ourselves i' the field; and to that end
Assemble we immediate council: Pompey
Thrives in our idleness.

LEPIDUS
To-morrow, Caesar,
I shall be furnish'd to inform you rightly
Both what by sea and land I can be able

To front this present time.

OCTAVIUS CAESAR
Till which encounter,
It is my business too. Farewell.

LEPIDUS
Farewell, my lord: what you shall know meantime
Of stirs abroad, I shall beseech you, sir,
To let me be partaker.

OCTAVIUS CAESAR
Doubt not, sir;
I knew it for my bond.

Exeunt

SCENE V. Alexandria. CLEOPATRA's palace.

Enter CLEOPATRA, CHARMIAN, IRAS, and MARDIAN

CLEOPATRA
Charmian!

CHARMIAN
Madam?

CLEOPATRA
Ha, ha!
Give me to drink mandragora.

CHARMIAN
Why, madam?

CLEOPATRA
That I might sleep out this great gap of time
My Antony is away.

CHARMIAN
You think of him too much.

CLEOPATRA
O, 'tis treason!

CHARMIAN
Madam, I trust, not so.

CLEOPATRA
Thou, eunuch Mardian!

MARDIAN
What's your highness' pleasure?

CLEOPATRA
Not now to hear thee sing; I take no pleasure

In aught an eunuch has: 'tis well for thee,
That, being unseminar'd, thy freer thoughts
May not fly forth of Egypt. Hast thou affections?

MARDIAN
Yes, gracious madam.

CLEOPATRA
Indeed!

MARDIAN
Not in deed, madam; for I can do nothing
But what indeed is honest to be done:
Yet have I fierce affections, and think
What Venus did with Mars.

CLEOPATRA
O Charmian,
Where think'st thou he is now? Stands he, or sits he?
Or does he walk? or is he on his horse?
O happy horse, to bear the weight of Antony!
Do bravely, horse! for wot'st thou whom thou movest?
The demi-Atlas of this earth, the arm
And burgonet of men. He's speaking now,
Or murmuring 'Where's my serpent of old Nile?'
For so he calls me: now I feed myself
With most delicious poison. Think on me,
That am with Phoebus' amorous pinches black,
And wrinkled deep in time? Broad-fronted Caesar,
When thou wast here above the ground, I was
A morsel for a monarch: and great Pompey
Would stand and make his eyes grow in my brow;
There would he anchor his aspect and die
With looking on his life.

Enter ALEXAS, from OCTAVIUS CAESAR

ALEXAS
Sovereign of Egypt, hail!

CLEOPATRA
How much unlike art thou Mark Antony!
Yet, coming from him, that great medicine hath
With his tinct gilded thee.
How goes it with my brave Mark Antony?

ALEXAS
Last thing he did, dear queen,
He kiss'd,--the last of many doubled kisses,--
This orient pearl. His speech sticks in my heart.

CLEOPATRA
Mine ear must pluck it thence.

ALEXAS
'Good friend,' quoth he,
'Say, the firm Roman to great Egypt sends
This treasure of an oyster; at whose foot,
To mend the petty present, I will piece
Her opulent throne with kingdoms; all the east,
Say thou, shall call her mistress.' So he nodded,
And soberly did mount an arm-gaunt steed,
Who neigh'd so high, that what I would have spoke
Was beastly dumb'd by him.

CLEOPATRA
What, was he sad or merry?

ALEXAS
Like to the time o' the year between the extremes
Of hot and cold, he was nor sad nor merry.

CLEOPATRA
O well-divided disposition! Note him,
Note him good Charmian, 'tis the man; but note him:
He was not sad, for he would shine on those
That make their looks by his; he was not merry,
Which seem'd to tell them his remembrance lay

In Egypt with his joy; but between both:
O heavenly mingle! Be'st thou sad or merry,
The violence of either thee becomes,
So does it no man else. Met'st thou my posts?

ALEXAS
Ay, madam, twenty several messengers:
Why do you send so thick?

CLEOPATRA
Who's born that day
When I forget to send to Antony,
Shall die a beggar. Ink and paper, Charmian.
Welcome, my good Alexas. Did I, Charmian,
Ever love Caesar so?

CHARMIAN
O that brave Caesar!

CLEOPATRA
Be choked with such another emphasis!
Say, the brave Antony.

CHARMIAN
The valiant Caesar!

CLEOPATRA
By Isis, I will give thee bloody teeth,
If thou with Caesar paragon again
My man of men.

CHARMIAN
By your most gracious pardon,
I sing but after you.

CLEOPATRA
My salad days,
When I was green in judgment: cold in blood,
To say as I said then! But, come, away;

Get me ink and paper:
He shall have every day a several greeting,
Or I'll unpeople Egypt.

Exeunt

ACT II

SCENE I. Messina. POMPEY's house.

Enter POMPEY, MENECRATES, and MENAS, in
warlike manner

POMPEY
If the great gods be just, they shall assist
The deeds of justest men.

MENECRATES
Know, worthy Pompey,
That what they do delay, they not deny.

POMPEY
Whiles we are suitors to their throne, decays
The thing we sue for.

MENECRATES
We, ignorant of ourselves,
Beg often our own harms, which the wise powers
Deny us for our good; so find we profit
By losing of our prayers.

POMPEY
I shall do well:
The people love me, and the sea is mine;
My powers are crescent, and my auguring hope
Says it will come to the full. Mark Antony
In Egypt sits at dinner, and will make
No wars without doors: Caesar gets money where
He loses hearts: Lepidus flatters both,
Of both is flatter'd; but he neither loves,
Nor either cares for him.

MENAS
Caesar and Lepidus
Are in the field: a mighty strength they carry.

POMPEY
Where have you this? 'tis false.

MENAS
From Silvius, sir.

POMPEY
He dreams: I know they are in Rome together,
Looking for Antony. But all the charms of love,
Salt Cleopatra, soften thy waned lip!
Let witchcraft join with beauty, lust with both!
Tie up the libertine in a field of feasts,
Keep his brain fuming; Epicurean cooks
Sharpen with cloyless sauce his appetite;
That sleep and feeding may prorogue his honour
Even till a Lethe'd dulness!

Enter VARRIUS

How now, Varrius!

VARRIUS
This is most certain that I shall deliver:
Mark Antony is every hour in Rome
Expected: since he went from Egypt 'tis
A space for further travel.

POMPEY
I could have given less matter
A better ear. Menas, I did not think
This amorous surfeiter would have donn'd his helm
For such a petty war: his soldiership
Is twice the other twain: but let us rear
The higher our opinion, that our stirring
Can from the lap of Egypt's widow pluck

The ne'er-lust-wearied Antony.

MENAS
I cannot hope
Caesar and Antony shall well greet together:
His wife that's dead did trespasses to Caesar;
His brother warr'd upon him; although, I think,
Not moved by Antony.

POMPEY
I know not, Menas,
How lesser enmities may give way to greater.
Were't not that we stand up against them all,
'Twere pregnant they should square between
themselves;
For they have entertained cause enough
To draw their swords: but how the fear of us
May cement their divisions and bind up
The petty difference, we yet not know.
Be't as our gods will have't! It only stands
Our lives upon to use our strongest hands.
Come, Menas.

Exeunt

SCENE II. Rome. The house of LEPIDUS.

Enter DOMITIUS ENOBARBUS and LEPIDUS

LEPIDUS
Good Enobarbus, 'tis a worthy deed,
And shall become you well, to entreat your captain
To soft and gentle speech.

DOMITIUS ENOBARBUS
I shall entreat him
To answer like himself: if Caesar move him,
Let Antony look over Caesar's head
And speak as loud as Mars. By Jupiter,
Were I the wearer of Antonius' beard,
I would not shave't to-day.

LEPIDUS
'Tis not a time
For private stomaching.

DOMITIUS ENOBARBUS
Every time
Serves for the matter that is then born in't.

LEPIDUS
But small to greater matters must give way.

DOMITIUS ENOBARBUS
Not if the small come first.

LEPIDUS
Your speech is passion:
But, pray you, stir no embers up. Here comes
The noble Antony.

Enter MARK ANTONY and VENTIDIUS

DOMITIUS ENOBARBUS
And yonder, Caesar.

Enter OCTAVIUS CAESAR, MECAENAS, and AGRIPPA

MARK ANTONY
If we compose well here, to Parthia:
Hark, Ventidius.

OCTAVIUS CAESAR
I do not know,
Mecaenas; ask Agrippa.

LEPIDUS
Noble friends,
That which combined us was most great, and let not
A leaner action rend us. What's amiss,
May it be gently heard: when we debate
Our trivial difference loud, we do commit
Murder in healing wounds: then, noble partners,
The rather, for I earnestly beseech,
Touch you the sourest points with sweetest terms,
Nor curstness grow to the matter.

MARK ANTONY
'Tis spoken well.
Were we before our armies, and to fight.
I should do thus.

Flourish

OCTAVIUS CAESAR
Welcome to Rome.

MARK ANTONY
Thank you.

OCTAVIUS CAESAR
Sit.

MARK ANTONY
Sit, sir.

OCTAVIUS CAESAR
Nay, then.

MARK ANTONY
I learn, you take things ill which are not so,
Or being, concern you not.

OCTAVIUS CAESAR
I must be laugh'd at,
If, or for nothing or a little, I
Should say myself offended, and with you
Chiefly i' the world; more laugh'd at, that I should
Once name you derogately, when to sound your name
It not concern'd me.

MARK ANTONY
My being in Egypt, Caesar,
What was't to you?

OCTAVIUS CAESAR
No more than my residing here at Rome
Might be to you in Egypt: yet, if you there
Did practise on my state, your being in Egypt
Might be my question.

MARK ANTONY
How intend you, practised?

OCTAVIUS CAESAR
You may be pleased to catch at mine intent
By what did here befal me. Your wife and brother
Made wars upon me; and their contestation
Was theme for you, you were the word of war.

MARK ANTONY
You do mistake your business; my brother never
Did urge me in his act: I did inquire it;
And have my learning from some true reports,
That drew their swords with you. Did he not rather
Discredit my authority with yours;
And make the wars alike against my stomach,
Having alike your cause? Of this my letters
Before did satisfy you. If you'll patch a quarrel,
As matter whole you have not to make it with,
It must not be with this.

OCTAVIUS CAESAR
You praise yourself
By laying defects of judgment to me; but
You patch'd up your excuses.

MARK ANTONY
Not so, not so;
I know you could not lack, I am certain on't,
Very necessity of this thought, that I,
Your partner in the cause 'gainst which he fought,
Could not with graceful eyes attend those wars
Which fronted mine own peace. As for my wife,
I would you had her spirit in such another:
The third o' the world is yours; which with a snaffle
You may pace easy, but not such a wife.

DOMITIUS ENOBARBUS
Would we had all such wives, that the men might go
to wars with the women!

MARK ANTONY
So much uncurbable, her garboils, Caesar
Made out of her impatience, which not wanted
Shrewdness of policy too, I grieving grant
Did you too much disquiet: for that you must
But say, I could not help it.

OCTAVIUS CAESAR
I wrote to you
When rioting in Alexandria; you
Did pocket up my letters, and with taunts
Did gibe my missive out of audience.

MARK ANTONY
Sir,
He fell upon me ere admitted: then
Three kings I had newly feasted, and did want
Of what I was i' the morning: but next day
I told him of myself; which was as much
As to have ask'd him pardon. Let this fellow
Be nothing of our strife; if we contend,
Out of our question wipe him.

OCTAVIUS CAESAR
You have broken
The article of your oath; which you shall never
Have tongue to charge me with.

LEPIDUS
Soft, Caesar!

MARK ANTONY
No,
Lepidus, let him speak:
The honour is sacred which he talks on now,
Supposing that I lack'd it. But, on, Caesar;
The article of my oath.

OCTAVIUS CAESAR
To lend me arms and aid when I required them;
The which you both denied.

MARK ANTONY
Neglected, rather;
And then when poison'd hours had bound me up
From mine own knowledge. As nearly as I may,

I'll play the penitent to you: but mine honesty
Shall not make poor my greatness, nor my power
Work without it. Truth is, that Fulvia,
To have me out of Egypt, made wars here;
For which myself, the ignorant motive, do
So far ask pardon as befits mine honour
To stoop in such a case.

LEPIDUS
'Tis noble spoken.

MECAENAS
If it might please you, to enforce no further
The griefs between ye: to forget them quite
Were to remember that the present need
Speaks to atone you.

LEPIDUS
Worthily spoken, Mecaenas.

DOMITIUS ENOBARBUS
Or, if you borrow one another's love for the
instant, you may, when you hear no more words of
Pompey, return it again: you shall have time to
wrangle in when you have nothing else to do.

MARK ANTONY
Thou art a soldier only: speak no more.

DOMITIUS ENOBARBUS
That truth should be silent I had almost forgot.

MARK ANTONY
You wrong this presence; therefore speak no more.

DOMITIUS ENOBARBUS
Go to, then; your considerate stone.

OCTAVIUS CAESAR
I do not much dislike the matter, but
The manner of his speech; for't cannot be
We shall remain in friendship, our conditions
So differing in their acts. Yet if I knew
What hoop should hold us stanch, from edge to edge
O' the world I would pursue it.

AGRIPPA
Give me leave, Caesar,--

OCTAVIUS CAESAR
Speak, Agrippa.

AGRIPPA
Thou hast a sister by the mother's side,
Admired Octavia: great Mark Antony
Is now a widower.

OCTAVIUS CAESAR
Say not so, Agrippa:
If Cleopatra heard you, your reproof
Were well deserved of rashness.

MARK ANTONY
I am not married, Caesar: let me hear
Agrippa further speak.

AGRIPPA
To hold you in perpetual amity,
To make you brothers, and to knit your hearts
With an unslipping knot, take Antony
Octavia to his wife; whose beauty claims
No worse a husband than the best of men;
Whose virtue and whose general graces speak
That which none else can utter. By this marriage,
All little jealousies, which now seem great,
And all great fears, which now import their dangers,
Would then be nothing: truths would be tales,

Where now half tales be truths: her love to both
Would, each to other and all loves to both,
Draw after her. Pardon what I have spoke;
For 'tis a studied, not a present thought,
By duty ruminated.

MARK ANTONY
Will Caesar speak?

OCTAVIUS CAESAR
Not till he hears how Antony is touch'd
With what is spoke already.

MARK ANTONY
What power is in Agrippa,
If I would say, 'Agrippa, be it so,'
To make this good?

OCTAVIUS CAESAR
The power of Caesar, and
His power unto Octavia.

MARK ANTONY
May I never
To this good purpose, that so fairly shows,
Dream of impediment! Let me have thy hand:
Further this act of grace: and from this hour
The heart of brothers govern in our loves
And sway our great designs!

OCTAVIUS CAESAR
There is my hand.
A sister I bequeath you, whom no brother
Did ever love so dearly: let her live
To join our kingdoms and our hearts; and never
Fly off our loves again!

LEPIDUS
Happily, amen!

MARK ANTONY
I did not think to draw my sword 'gainst Pompey;
For he hath laid strange courtesies and great
Of late upon me: I must thank him only,
Lest my remembrance suffer ill report;
At heel of that, defy him.

LEPIDUS
Time calls upon's:
Of us must Pompey presently be sought,
Or else he seeks out us.

MARK ANTONY
Where lies he?

OCTAVIUS CAESAR
About the mount Misenum.

MARK ANTONY
What is his strength by land?

OCTAVIUS CAESAR
Great and increasing: but by sea
He is an absolute master.

MARK ANTONY
So is the fame.
Would we had spoke together! Haste we for it:
Yet, ere we put ourselves in arms, dispatch we
The business we have talk'd of.

OCTAVIUS CAESAR
With most gladness:
And do invite you to my sister's view,
Whither straight I'll lead you.

MARK ANTONY
Let us, Lepidus,

Not lack your company.

LEPIDUS
Noble Antony,
Not sickness should detain me.

Flourish. Exeunt OCTAVIUS CAESAR, MARK
ANTONY, and LEPIDUS

MECAENAS
Welcome from Egypt, sir.

DOMITIUS ENOBARBUS
Half the heart of Caesar, worthy Mecaenas! My
honourable friend, Agrippa!

AGRIPPA
Good Enobarbus!

MECAENAS
We have cause to be glad that matters are so well
digested. You stayed well by 't in Egypt.

DOMITIUS ENOBARBUS
Ay, sir; we did sleep day out of countenance, and
made the night light with drinking.

MECAENAS
Eight wild-boars roasted whole at a breakfast, and
but twelve persons there; is this true?

DOMITIUS ENOBARBUS
This was but as a fly by an eagle: we had much more
monstrous matter of feast, which worthily deserved
noting.

MECAENAS
She's a most triumphant lady, if report be square to
her.

DOMITIUS ENOBARBUS
When she first met Mark Antony, she pursed up
his heart, upon the river of Cydnus.

AGRIPPA
There she appeared indeed; or my reporter devised
well for her.

DOMITIUS ENOBARBUS
I will tell you.
The barge she sat in, like a burnish'd throne,
Burn'd on the water: the poop was beaten gold;
Purple the sails, and so perfumed that
The winds were love-sick with them; the oars were
silver,
Which to the tune of flutes kept stroke, and made
The water which they beat to follow faster,
As amorous of their strokes. For her own person,
It beggar'd all description: she did lie
In her pavilion--cloth-of-gold of tissue--
O'er-picturing that Venus where we see
The fancy outwork nature: on each side her
Stood pretty dimpled boys, like smiling Cupids,
With divers-colour'd fans, whose wind did seem
To glow the delicate cheeks which they did cool,
And what they undid did.

AGRIPPA
O, rare for Antony!

DOMITIUS ENOBARBUS
Her gentlewomen, like the Nereides,
So many mermaids, tended her i' the eyes,
And made their bends adornings: at the helm
A seeming mermaid steers: the silken tackle
Swell with the touches of those flower-soft hands,
That yarely frame the office. From the barge
A strange invisible perfume hits the sense

Of the adjacent wharfs. The city cast
Her people out upon her; and Antony,
Enthroned i' the market-place, did sit alone,
Whistling to the air; which, but for vacancy,
Had gone to gaze on Cleopatra too,
And made a gap in nature.

AGRIPPA
Rare Egyptian!

DOMITIUS ENOBARBUS
Upon her landing, Antony sent to her,
Invited her to supper: she replied,
It should be better he became her guest;
Which she entreated: our courteous Antony,
Whom ne'er the word of 'No' woman heard speak,
Being barber'd ten times o'er, goes to the feast,
And for his ordinary pays his heart
For what his eyes eat only.

AGRIPPA
Royal wench!
She made great Caesar lay his sword to bed:
He plough'd her, and she cropp'd.

DOMITIUS ENOBARBUS
I saw her once
Hop forty paces through the public street;
And having lost her breath, she spoke, and panted,
That she did make defect perfection,
And, breathless, power breathe forth.

MECAENAS
Now Antony must leave her utterly.

DOMITIUS ENOBARBUS
Never; he will not:
Age cannot wither her, nor custom stale
Her infinite variety: other women cloy

The appetites they feed: but she makes hungry
Where most she satisfies; for vilest things
Become themselves in her: that the holy priests
Bless her when she is riggish.

MECAENAS
If beauty, wisdom, modesty, can settle
The heart of Antony, Octavia is
A blessed lottery to him.

AGRIPPA
Let us go.
Good Enobarbus, make yourself my guest
Whilst you abide here.

DOMITIUS ENOBARBUS
Humbly, sir, I thank you.

Exeunt

SCENE III. The same. OCTAVIUS CAESAR's house.

Enter MARK ANTONY, OCTAVIUS CAESAR, OCTAVIA
between them, and Attendants

MARK ANTONY
The world and my great office will sometimes
Divide me from your bosom.

OCTAVIA
All which time
Before the gods my knee shall bow my prayers
To them for you.

MARK ANTONY
Good night, sir. My Octavia,
Read not my blemishes in the world's report:
I have not kept my square; but that to come
Shall all be done by the rule. Good night, dear lady.
Good night, sir.

OCTAVIUS CAESAR
Good night.

Exeunt OCTAVIUS CAESAR and OCTAVIA

Enter Soothsayer

MARK ANTONY
Now, sirrah; you do wish yourself in Egypt?

Soothsayer
Would I had never come from thence, nor you Thither!

MARK ANTONY
If you can, your reason?

Soothsayer
I see it in
My motion, have it not in my tongue: but yet
Hie you to Egypt again.

MARK ANTONY
Say to me,
Whose fortunes shall rise higher, Caesar's or mine?

Soothsayer
Caesar's.
Therefore, O Antony, stay not by his side:
Thy demon, that's thy spirit which keeps thee, is
Noble, courageous high, unmatchable,
Where Caesar's is not; but, near him, thy angel
Becomes a fear, as being o'erpower'd: therefore
Make space enough between you.

MARK ANTONY
Speak this no more.

Soothsayer
To none but thee; no more, but when to thee.
If thou dost play with him at any game,
Thou art sure to lose; and, of that natural luck,
He beats thee 'gainst the odds: thy lustre thickens,
When he shines by: I say again, thy spirit
Is all afraid to govern thee near him;
But, he away, 'tis noble.

MARK ANTONY
Get thee gone:
Say to Ventidius I would speak with him:

Exit Soothsayer

He shall to Parthia. Be it art or hap,
He hath spoken true: the very dice obey him;
And in our sports my better cunning faints

Under his chance: if we draw lots, he speeds;
His cocks do win the battle still of mine,
When it is all to nought; and his quails ever
Beat mine, inhoop'd, at odds. I will to Egypt:
And though I make this marriage for my peace,
I' the east my pleasure lies.

Enter VENTIDIUS

O, come, Ventidius,
You must to Parthia: your commission's ready;
Follow me, and receive't.

Exeunt

SCENE IV. The same. A street.

Enter LEPIDUS, MECAENAS, and AGRIPPA

LEPIDUS
Trouble yourselves no further: pray you, hasten
Your generals after.

AGRIPPA
Sir, Mark Antony
Will e'en but kiss Octavia, and we'll follow.

LEPIDUS
Till I shall see you in your soldier's dress,
Which will become you both, farewell.

MECAENAS
We shall,
As I conceive the journey, be at the Mount
Before you, Lepidus.

LEPIDUS
Your way is shorter;
My purposes do draw me much about:
You'll win two days upon me.

MECAENAS AGRIPPA
Sir, good success!

LEPIDUS
Farewell.

Exeunt

SCENE V. Alexandria. CLEOPATRA's palace.

Enter CLEOPATRA, CHARMIAN, IRAS, and ALEXAS

CLEOPATRA
Give me some music; music, moody food
Of us that trade in love.

Attendants
The music, ho!

Enter MARDIAN

CLEOPATRA
Let it alone; let's to billiards: come, Charmian.

CHARMIAN
My arm is sore; best play with Mardian.

CLEOPATRA
As well a woman with an eunuch play'd
As with a woman. Come, you'll play with me, sir?

MARDIAN
As well as I can, madam.

CLEOPATRA
And when good will is show'd, though't come
too short,
The actor may plead pardon. I'll none now:
Give me mine angle; we'll to the river: there,
My music playing far off, I will betray
Tawny-finn'd fishes; my bended hook shall pierce
Their slimy jaws; and, as I draw them up,
I'll think them every one an Antony,
And say 'Ah, ha! you're caught.'

CHARMIAN
'Twas merry when
You wager'd on your angling; when your diver
Did hang a salt-fish on his hook, which he
With fervency drew up.

CLEOPATRA
That time,--O times!--
I laugh'd him out of patience; and that night
I laugh'd him into patience; and next morn,
Ere the ninth hour, I drunk him to his bed;
Then put my tires and mantles on him, whilst
I wore his sword Philippan.

Enter a Messenger

O, from Italy
Ram thou thy fruitful tidings in mine ears,
That long time have been barren.

Messenger
Madam, madam,--

CLEOPATRA
Antonius dead!--If thou say so, villain,
Thou kill'st thy mistress: but well and free,
If thou so yield him, there is gold, and here
My bluest veins to kiss; a hand that kings
Have lipp'd, and trembled kissing.

Messenger
First, madam, he is well.

CLEOPATRA
Why, there's more gold.
But, sirrah, mark, we use
To say the dead are well: bring it to that,
The gold I give thee will I melt and pour
Down thy ill-uttering throat.

Messenger
Good madam, hear me.

CLEOPATRA
Well, go to, I will;
But there's no goodness in thy face: if Antony
Be free and healthful,--so tart a favour
To trumpet such good tidings! If not well,
Thou shouldst come like a Fury crown'd with snakes,
Not like a formal man.

Messenger
Will't please you hear me?

CLEOPATRA
I have a mind to strike thee ere thou speak'st:
Yet if thou say Antony lives, is well,
Or friends with Caesar, or not captive to him,
I'll set thee in a shower of gold, and hail
Rich pearls upon thee.

Messenger
Madam, he's well.

CLEOPATRA
Well said.

Messenger
And friends with Caesar.

CLEOPATRA
Thou'rt an honest man.

Messenger
Caesar and he are greater friends than ever.

CLEOPATRA
Make thee a fortune from me.

Messenger
But yet, madam,--

CLEOPATRA
I do not like 'But yet,' it does allay
The good precedence; fie upon 'But yet'!
'But yet' is as a gaoler to bring forth
Some monstrous malefactor. Prithee, friend,
Pour out the pack of matter to mine ear,
The good and bad together: he's friends with Caesar:
In state of health thou say'st; and thou say'st free.

Messenger
Free, madam! no; I made no such report:
He's bound unto Octavia.

CLEOPATRA
For what good turn?

Messenger
For the best turn i' the bed.

CLEOPATRA
I am pale, Charmian.

Messenger
Madam, he's married to Octavia.

CLEOPATRA
The most infectious pestilence upon thee!

Strikes him down

Messenger
Good madam, patience.

CLEOPATRA
What say you? Hence,

Strikes him again

Horrible villain! or I'll spurn thine eyes
Like balls before me; I'll unhair thy head:

She hales him up and down

Thou shalt be whipp'd with wire, and stew'd in brine,
Smarting in lingering pickle.

Messenger
Gracious madam,
I that do bring the news made not the match.

CLEOPATRA
Say 'tis not so, a province I will give thee,
And make thy fortunes proud: the blow thou hadst
Shall make thy peace for moving me to rage;
And I will boot thee with what gift beside
Thy modesty can beg.

Messenger
He's married, madam.

CLEOPATRA
Rogue, thou hast lived too long.

Draws a knife

Messenger
Nay, then I'll run.
What mean you, madam? I have made no fault.

Exit

CHARMIAN
Good madam, keep yourself within yourself:
The man is innocent.

CLEOPATRA
Some innocents 'scape not the thunderbolt.
Melt Egypt into Nile! and kindly creatures
Turn all to serpents! Call the slave again:
Though I am mad, I will not bite him: call.

CHARMIAN
He is afeard to come.

CLEOPATRA
I will not hurt him.

Exit CHARMIAN

These hands do lack nobility, that they strike
A meaner than myself; since I myself
Have given myself the cause.

Re-enter CHARMIAN and Messenger

Come hither, sir.
Though it be honest, it is never good
To bring bad news: give to a gracious message.
An host of tongues; but let ill tidings tell
Themselves when they be felt.

Messenger
I have done my duty.

CLEOPATRA
Is he married?
I cannot hate thee worser than I do,
If thou again say 'Yes.'

Messenger
He's married, madam.

CLEOPATRA

The gods confound thee! dost thou hold there still?

Messenger
Should I lie, madam?

CLEOPATRA
O, I would thou didst,
So half my Egypt were submerged and made
A cistern for scaled snakes! Go, get thee hence:
Hadst thou Narcissus in thy face, to me
Thou wouldst appear most ugly. He is married?

Messenger
I crave your highness' pardon.

CLEOPATRA
He is married?

Messenger
Take no offence that I would not offend you:
To punish me for what you make me do.
Seems much unequal: he's married to Octavia.

CLEOPATRA
O, that his fault should make a knave of thee,
That art not what thou'rt sure of! Get thee hence:
The merchandise which thou hast brought from Rome
Are all too dear for me: lie they upon thy hand,
And be undone by 'em!

Exit Messenger

CHARMIAN
Good your highness, patience.

CLEOPATRA
In praising Antony, I have dispraised Caesar.

CHARMIAN

Many times, madam.

CLEOPATRA
I am paid for't now.
Lead me from hence:
I faint: O Iras, Charmian! 'tis no matter.
Go to the fellow, good Alexas; bid him
Report the feature of Octavia, her years,
Her inclination, let him not leave out
The colour of her hair: bring me word quickly.

Exit ALEXAS

Let him for ever go:--let him not--Charmian,
Though he be painted one way like a Gorgon,
The other way's a Mars. Bid you Alexas

To MARDIAN

Bring me word how tall she is. Pity me, Charmian,
But do not speak to me. Lead me to my chamber.

Exeunt

SCENE VI. Near Misenum.

Flourish. Enter POMPEY and MENAS at one door,
with drum and trumpet: at another, OCTAVIUS
CAESAR, MARK ANTONY, LEPIDUS, DOMITIUS
ENOBARBUS, MECAENAS, with Soldiers marching

POMPEY
Your hostages I have, so have you mine;
And we shall talk before we fight.

OCTAVIUS CAESAR
Most meet
That first we come to words; and therefore have we
Our written purposes before us sent;
Which, if thou hast consider'd, let us know
If 'twill tie up thy discontented sword,
And carry back to Sicily much tall youth
That else must perish here.

POMPEY
To you all three,
The senators alone of this great world,
Chief factors for the gods, I do not know
Wherefore my father should revengers want,
Having a son and friends; since Julius Caesar,
Who at Philippi the good Brutus ghosted,
There saw you labouring for him. What was't
That moved pale Cassius to conspire; and what
Made the all-honour'd, honest Roman, Brutus,
With the arm'd rest, courtiers and beauteous freedom,
To drench the Capitol; but that they would
Have one man but a man? And that is it
Hath made me rig my navy; at whose burthen
The anger'd ocean foams; with which I meant
To scourge the ingratitude that despiteful Rome
Cast on my noble father.

OCTAVIUS CAESAR
Take your time.

MARK ANTONY
Thou canst not fear us, Pompey, with thy sails;
We'll speak with thee at sea: at land, thou know'st
How much we do o'er-count thee.

POMPEY
At land, indeed,
Thou dost o'er-count me of my father's house:
But, since the cuckoo builds not for himself,
Remain in't as thou mayst.

LEPIDUS
Be pleased to tell us--
For this is from the present--how you take
The offers we have sent you.

OCTAVIUS CAESAR
There's the point.

MARK ANTONY
Which do not be entreated to, but weigh
What it is worth embraced.

OCTAVIUS CAESAR
And what may follow,
To try a larger fortune.

POMPEY
You have made me offer
Of Sicily, Sardinia; and I must
Rid all the sea of pirates; then, to send
Measures of wheat to Rome; this 'greed upon
To part with unhack'd edges, and bear back
Our targes undinted.

OCTAVIUS CAESAR MARK ANTONY LEPIDUS
That's our offer.

POMPEY
Know, then,
I came before you here a man prepared
To take this offer: but Mark Antony
Put me to some impatience: though I lose
The praise of it by telling, you must know,
When Caesar and your brother were at blows,
Your mother came to Sicily and did find
Her welcome friendly.

MARK ANTONY
I have heard it, Pompey;
And am well studied for a liberal thanks
Which I do owe you.

POMPEY
Let me have your hand:
I did not think, sir, to have met you here.

MARK ANTONY
The beds i' the east are soft; and thanks to you,
That call'd me timelier than my purpose hither;
For I have gain'd by 't.

OCTAVIUS CAESAR
Since I saw you last,
There is a change upon you.

POMPEY
Well, I know not
What counts harsh fortune casts upon my face;
But in my bosom shall she never come,
To make my heart her vassal.

LEPIDUS
Well met here.

POMPEY
I hope so, Lepidus. Thus we are agreed:
I crave our composition may be written,
And seal'd between us.

OCTAVIUS CAESAR
That's the next to do.

POMPEY
We'll feast each other ere we part; and let's
Draw lots who shall begin.

MARK ANTONY
That will I, Pompey.

POMPEY
No, Antony, take the lot: but, first
Or last, your fine Egyptian cookery
Shall have the fame. I have heard that Julius Caesar
Grew fat with feasting there.

MARK ANTONY
You have heard much.

POMPEY
I have fair meanings, sir.

MARK ANTONY
And fair words to them.

POMPEY
Then so much have I heard:
And I have heard, Apollodorus carried--

DOMITIUS ENOBARBUS
No more of that: he did so.

POMPEY
What, I pray you?

DOMITIUS ENOBARBUS
A certain queen to Caesar in a mattress.

POMPEY
I know thee now: how farest thou, soldier?

DOMITIUS ENOBARBUS
Well;
And well am like to do; for, I perceive,
Four feasts are toward.

POMPEY
Let me shake thy hand;
I never hated thee: I have seen thee fight,
When I have envied thy behavior.

DOMITIUS ENOBARBUS
Sir,
I never loved you much; but I ha' praised ye,
When you have well deserved ten times as much
As I have said you did.

POMPEY
Enjoy thy plainness,
It nothing ill becomes thee.
Aboard my galley I invite you all:
Will you lead, lords?

OCTAVIUS CAESAR MARK ANTONY LEPIDUS
Show us the way, sir.

POMPEY
Come.

Exeunt all but MENAS and ENOBARBUS

MENAS
[Aside] Thy father, Pompey, would ne'er have
made this treaty.--You and I have known, sir.

DOMITIUS ENOBARBUS
At sea, I think.

MENAS
We have, sir.

DOMITIUS ENOBARBUS
You have done well by water.

MENAS
And you by land.

DOMITIUS ENOBARBUS
I will praise any man that will praise me; though it
cannot be denied what I have done by land.

MENAS
Nor what I have done by water.

DOMITIUS ENOBARBUS
Yes, something you can deny for your own
safety: you have been a great thief by sea.

MENAS
And you by land.

DOMITIUS ENOBARBUS
There I deny my land service. But give me your
hand, Menas: if our eyes had authority, here they
might take two thieves kissing.

MENAS
All men's faces are true, whatsome'er their hands are.

DOMITIUS ENOBARBUS
But there is never a fair woman has a true face.

MENAS
No slander; they steal hearts.

DOMITIUS ENOBARBUS
We came hither to fight with you.

MENAS
For my part, I am sorry it is turned to a drinking.
Pompey doth this day laugh away his fortune.

DOMITIUS ENOBARBUS
If he do, sure, he cannot weep't back again.

MENAS
You've said, sir. We looked not for Mark Antony
here: pray you, is he married to Cleopatra?

DOMITIUS ENOBARBUS
Caesar's sister is called Octavia.

MENAS
True, sir; she was the wife of Caius Marcellus.

DOMITIUS ENOBARBUS
But she is now the wife of Marcus Antonius.

MENAS
Pray ye, sir?

DOMITIUS ENOBARBUS
'Tis true.

MENAS
Then is Caesar and he for ever knit together.

DOMITIUS ENOBARBUS
If I were bound to divine of this unity, I would
not prophesy so.

MENAS
I think the policy of that purpose made more in the
marriage than the love of the parties.

DOMITIUS ENOBARBUS
I think so too. But you shall find, the band that
seems to tie their friendship together will be the
very strangler of their amity: Octavia is of a
holy, cold, and still conversation.

MENAS
Who would not have his wife so?

DOMITIUS ENOBARBUS
Not he that himself is not so; which is Mark Antony.
He will to his Egyptian dish again: then shall the
sighs of Octavia blow the fire up in Caesar; and, as
I said before, that which is the strength of their
amity shall prove the immediate author of their
variance. Antony will use his affection where it is:
he married but his occasion here.

MENAS
And thus it may be. Come, sir, will you aboard?
I have a health for you.

DOMITIUS ENOBARBUS
I shall take it, sir: we have used our throats in Egypt.

MENAS
Come, let's away.

Exeunt

SCENE VII. On board POMPEY's galley, off Misenum.

Music plays. Enter two or three Servants with a banquet

First Servant
Here they'll be, man. Some o' their plants are
ill-rooted already: the least wind i' the world
will blow them down.

Second Servant
Lepidus is high-coloured.

First Servant
They have made him drink alms-drink.

Second Servant
As they pinch one another by the disposition, he
cries out 'No more;' reconciles them to his
entreaty, and himself to the drink.

First Servant
But it raises the greater war between him and
his discretion.

Second Servant
Why, this is to have a name in great men's
fellowship: I had as lief have a reed that will do
me no service as a partisan I could not heave.

First Servant
To be called into a huge sphere, and not to be seen
to move in't, are the holes where eyes should be,
which pitifully disaster the cheeks.

A sennet sounded. Enter OCTAVIUS CAESAR, MARK
ANTONY, LEPIDUS, POMPEY, AGRIPPA, MECAENAS,
DOMITIUS ENOBARBUS, MENAS, with other captains

MARK ANTONY
[To OCTAVIUS CAESAR] Thus do they, sir: they take
the flow o' the Nile
By certain scales i' the pyramid; they know,
By the height, the lowness, or the mean, if dearth
Or foison follow: the higher Nilus swells,
The more it promises: as it ebbs, the seedsman
Upon the slime and ooze scatters his grain,
And shortly comes to harvest.

LEPIDUS
You've strange serpents there.

MARK ANTONY
Ay, Lepidus.

LEPIDUS
Your serpent of Egypt is bred now of your mud by the
operation of your sun: so is your crocodile.

MARK ANTONY
They are so.

POMPEY
Sit,--and some wine! A health to Lepidus!

LEPIDUS
I am not so well as I should be, but I'll ne'er out.

DOMITIUS ENOBARBUS
Not till you have slept; I fear me you'll be in till then.

LEPIDUS
Nay, certainly, I have heard the Ptolemies'
pyramises are very goodly things; without

contradiction, I have heard that.

MENAS
[Aside to POMPEY] Pompey, a word.

POMPEY
[Aside to MENAS] Say in mine ear:
what is't?

MENAS
[Aside to POMPEY] Forsake thy seat, I do beseech
thee, captain,
And hear me speak a word.

POMPEY
[Aside to MENAS] Forbear me till anon.
This wine for Lepidus!

LEPIDUS
What manner o' thing is your crocodile?

MARK ANTONY
It is shaped, sir, like itself; and it is as broad
as it hath breadth: it is just so high as it is,
and moves with its own organs: it lives by that
which nourisheth it; and the elements once out of
it, it transmigrates.

LEPIDUS
What colour is it of?

MARK ANTONY
Of it own colour too.

LEPIDUS
'Tis a strange serpent.

MARK ANTONY
'Tis so. And the tears of it are wet.

OCTAVIUS CAESAR
Will this description satisfy him?

MARK ANTONY
With the health that Pompey gives him, else he is a
very epicure.

POMPEY
[Aside to MENAS] Go hang, sir, hang! Tell me of
that? away!
Do as I bid you. Where's this cup I call'd for?

MENAS
[Aside to POMPEY] If for the sake of merit thou
wilt hear me,
Rise from thy stool.

POMPEY
[Aside to MENAS] I think thou'rt mad.
The matter?

Rises, and walks aside

MENAS
I have ever held my cap off to thy fortunes.

POMPEY
Thou hast served me with much faith. What's else to
say?
Be jolly, lords.

MARK ANTONY
These quick-sands, Lepidus,
Keep off them, for you sink.

MENAS
Wilt thou be lord of all the world?

POMPEY
What say'st thou?

MENAS
Wilt thou be lord of the whole world? That's twice.

POMPEY
How should that be?

MENAS
But entertain it,
And, though thou think me poor, I am the man
Will give thee all the world.

POMPEY
Hast thou drunk well?

MENAS
Now, Pompey, I have kept me from the cup.
Thou art, if thou darest be, the earthly Jove:
Whate'er the ocean pales, or sky inclips,
Is thine, if thou wilt ha't.

POMPEY
Show me which way.

MENAS
These three world-sharers, these competitors,
Are in thy vessel: let me cut the cable;
And, when we are put off, fall to their throats:
All there is thine.

POMPEY
Ah, this thou shouldst have done,
And not have spoke on't! In me 'tis villany;
In thee't had been good service. Thou must know,
'Tis not my profit that does lead mine honour;
Mine honour, it. Repent that e'er thy tongue
Hath so betray'd thine act: being done unknown,

I should have found it afterwards well done;
But must condemn it now. Desist, and drink.

MENAS
[Aside] For this,
I'll never follow thy pall'd fortunes more.
Who seeks, and will not take when once 'tis offer'd,
Shall never find it more.

POMPEY
This health to Lepidus!

MARK ANTONY
Bear him ashore. I'll pledge it for him, Pompey.

DOMITIUS ENOBARBUS
Here's to thee, Menas!

MENAS
Enobarbus, welcome!

POMPEY
Fill till the cup be hid.

DOMITIUS ENOBARBUS
There's a strong fellow, Menas.

Pointing to the Attendant who carries off LEPIDUS

MENAS
Why?

DOMITIUS ENOBARBUS
A' bears the third part of the world, man; see'st
not?

MENAS
The third part, then, is drunk: would it were all,
That it might go on wheels!

DOMITIUS ENOBARBUS
Drink thou; increase the reels.

MENAS
Come.

POMPEY
This is not yet an Alexandrian feast.

MARK ANTONY
It ripens towards it. Strike the vessels, ho?
Here is to Caesar!

OCTAVIUS CAESAR
I could well forbear't.
It's monstrous labour, when I wash my brain,
And it grows fouler.

MARK ANTONY
Be a child o' the time.

OCTAVIUS CAESAR
Possess it, I'll make answer:
But I had rather fast from all four days
Than drink so much in one.

DOMITIUS ENOBARBUS
Ha, my brave emperor!

To MARK ANTONY

Shall we dance now the Egyptian Bacchanals,
And celebrate our drink?

POMPEY
Let's ha't, good soldier.

MARK ANTONY
Come, let's all take hands,
Till that the conquering wine hath steep'd our sense
In soft and delicate Lethe.

DOMITIUS ENOBARBUS
All take hands.
Make battery to our ears with the loud music:
The while I'll place you: then the boy shall sing;
The holding every man shall bear as loud
As his strong sides can volley.

Music plays. DOMITIUS ENOBARBUS places them
hand in hand

THE SONG.
Come, thou monarch of the vine,
Plumpy Bacchus with pink eyne!
In thy fats our cares be drown'd,
With thy grapes our hairs be crown'd:
Cup us, till the world go round,
Cup us, till the world go round!

OCTAVIUS CAESAR
What would you more? Pompey, good night. Good
brother,
Let me request you off: our graver business
Frowns at this levity. Gentle lords, let's part;
You see we have burnt our cheeks: strong Enobarb
Is weaker than the wine; and mine own tongue
Splits what it speaks: the wild disguise hath almost
Antick'd us all. What needs more words? Good night.
Good Antony, your hand.

POMPEY
I'll try you on the shore.

MARK ANTONY
And shall, sir; give's your hand.

POMPEY
O Antony,
You have my father's house,--But, what? we are
friends.
Come, down into the boat.

DOMITIUS ENOBARBUS
Take heed you fall not.

Exeunt all but DOMITIUS ENOBARBUS and MENAS

Menas, I'll not on shore.

MENAS
No, to my cabin.
These drums! these trumpets, flutes! what!
Let Neptune hear we bid a loud farewell
To these great fellows: sound and be hang'd, sound
out!

Sound a flourish, with drums

DOMITIUS ENOBARBUS
Ho! says a' There's my cap.

MENAS
Ho! Noble captain, come.

Exeunt

ACT III

SCENE I. A plain in Syria.

*Enter VENTIDIUS as it were in triumph, with SILIUS,
and other Romans, Officers, and Soldiers; the dead
body of PACORUS borne before him*

VENTIDIUS
Now, darting Parthia, art thou struck; and now
Pleased fortune does of Marcus Crassus' death
Make me revenger. Bear the king's son's body
Before our army. Thy Pacorus, Orodes,
Pays this for Marcus Crassus.

SILIUS
Noble Ventidius,
Whilst yet with Parthian blood thy sword is warm,
The fugitive Parthians follow; spur through Media,
Mesopotamia, and the shelters whither
The routed fly: so thy grand captain Antony
Shall set thee on triumphant chariots and
Put garlands on thy head.

VENTIDIUS
O Silius, Silius,
I have done enough; a lower place, note well,
May make too great an act: for learn this, Silius;
Better to leave undone, than by our deed
Acquire too high a fame when him we serve's away.
Caesar and Antony have ever won
More in their officer than person: Sossius,
One of my place in Syria, his lieutenant,
For quick accumulation of renown,
Which he achieved by the minute, lost his favour.
Who does i' the wars more than his captain can
Becomes his captain's captain: and ambition,

The soldier's virtue, rather makes choice of loss,
Than gain which darkens him.
I could do more to do Antonius good,
But 'twould offend him; and in his offence
Should my performance perish.

SILIUS
Thou hast, Ventidius,
that
Without the which a soldier, and his sword,
Grants scarce distinction. Thou wilt write to Antony!

VENTIDIUS
I'll humbly signify what in his name,
That magical word of war, we have effected;
How, with his banners and his well-paid ranks,
The ne'er-yet-beaten horse of Parthia
We have jaded out o' the field.

SILIUS
Where is he now?

VENTIDIUS
He purposeth to Athens: whither, with what haste
The weight we must convey with's will permit,
We shall appear before him. On there; pass along!

Exeunt

SCENE II. Rome. An ante-chamber in OCTAVIUS CAESAR's house.

Enter AGRIPPA at one door, DOMITIUS ENOBARBUS at another

AGRIPPA
What, are the brothers parted?

DOMITIUS ENOBARBUS
They have dispatch'd with Pompey, he is gone;
The other three are sealing. Octavia weeps
To part from Rome; Caesar is sad; and Lepidus,
Since Pompey's feast, as Menas says, is troubled
With the green sickness.

AGRIPPA
'Tis a noble Lepidus.

DOMITIUS ENOBARBUS
A very fine one: O, how he loves Caesar!

AGRIPPA
Nay, but how dearly he adores Mark Antony!

DOMITIUS ENOBARBUS
Caesar? Why, he's the Jupiter of men.

AGRIPPA
What's Antony? The god of Jupiter.

DOMITIUS ENOBARBUS
Spake you of Caesar? How! the non-pareil!

AGRIPPA
O Antony! O thou Arabian bird!

DOMITIUS ENOBARBUS
Would you praise Caesar, say 'Caesar:' go no further.

AGRIPPA
Indeed, he plied them both with excellent praises.

DOMITIUS ENOBARBUS
But he loves Caesar best; yet he loves Antony:
Ho! hearts, tongues, figures, scribes, bards,
poets, cannot
Think, speak, cast, write, sing, number, ho!
His love to Antony. But as for Caesar,
Kneel down, kneel down, and wonder.

AGRIPPA
Both he loves.

DOMITIUS ENOBARBUS
They are his shards, and he their beetle.

Trumpets within

So;
This is to horse. Adieu, noble Agrippa.

AGRIPPA
Good fortune, worthy soldier; and farewell.

Enter OCTAVIUS CAESAR, MARK ANTONY, LEPIDUS,
and OCTAVIA

MARK ANTONY
No further, sir.

OCTAVIUS CAESAR
You take from me a great part of myself;
Use me well in 't. Sister, prove such a wife
As my thoughts make thee, and as my farthest band
Shall pass on thy approof. Most noble Antony,

Let not the piece of virtue, which is set
Betwixt us as the cement of our love,
To keep it builded, be the ram to batter
The fortress of it; for better might we
Have loved without this mean, if on both parts
This be not cherish'd.

MARK ANTONY
Make me not offended
In your distrust.

OCTAVIUS CAESAR
I have said.

MARK ANTONY
You shall not find,
Though you be therein curious, the least cause
For what you seem to fear: so, the gods keep you,
And make the hearts of Romans serve your ends!
We will here part.

OCTAVIUS CAESAR
Farewell, my dearest sister, fare thee well:
The elements be kind to thee, and make
Thy spirits all of comfort! fare thee well.

OCTAVIA
My noble brother!

MARK ANTONY
The April 's in her eyes: it is love's spring,
And these the showers to bring it on. Be cheerful.

OCTAVIA
Sir, look well to my husband's house; and--

OCTAVIUS CAESAR
What, Octavia?

OCTAVIA
I'll tell you in your ear.

MARK ANTONY
Her tongue will not obey her heart, nor can
Her heart inform her tongue,--the swan's
down-feather,
That stands upon the swell at full of tide,
And neither way inclines.

DOMITIUS ENOBARBUS
[Aside to AGRIPPA] Will Caesar weep?

AGRIPPA
[Aside to DOMITIUS ENOBARBUS] He has a cloud in
's face.

DOMITIUS ENOBARBUS
[Aside to AGRIPPA] He were the worse for that,
were he a horse;
So is he, being a man.

AGRIPPA
[Aside to DOMITIUS ENOBARBUS] Why, Enobarbus,
When Antony found Julius Caesar dead,
He cried almost to roaring; and he wept
When at Philippi he found Brutus slain.

DOMITIUS ENOBARBUS
[Aside to AGRIPPA] That year, indeed, he was
troubled with a rheum;
What willingly he did confound he wail'd,
Believe't, till I wept too.

OCTAVIUS CAESAR
No, sweet Octavia,
You shall hear from me still; the time shall not
Out-go my thinking on you.

MARK ANTONY
Come, sir, come;
I'll wrestle with you in my strength of love:
Look, here I have you; thus I let you go,
And give you to the gods.

OCTAVIUS CAESAR
Adieu; be happy!

LEPIDUS
Let all the number of the stars give light
To thy fair way!

OCTAVIUS CAESAR
Farewell, fa rewell!

Kisses OCTAVIA

MARK ANTONY
Farewell!

Trumpets sound. Exeunt

SCENE III. Alexandria. CLEOPATRA's palace.

Enter CLEOPATRA, CHARMIAN, IRAS, and ALEXAS

CLEOPATRA
Where is the fellow?

ALEXAS
Half afeard to come.

CLEOPATRA
Go to, go to.

Enter the Messenger as before

Come hither, sir.

ALEXAS
Good majesty,
Herod of Jewry dare not look upon you
But when you are well pleased.

CLEOPATRA
That Herod's head
I'll have: but how, when Antony is gone
Through whom I might command it? Come thou near.

Messenger
Most gracious majesty,--

CLEOPATRA
Didst thou behold Octavia?

Messenger
Ay, dread queen.

CLEOPATRA
Where?

Messenger
Madam, in Rome;
I look'd her in the face, and saw her led
Between her brother and Mark Antony.

CLEOPATRA
Is she as tall as me?

Messenger
She is not, madam.

CLEOPATRA
Didst hear her speak? is she shrill-tongued or low?

Messenger
Madam, I heard her speak; she is low-voiced.

CLEOPATRA
That's not so good: he cannot like her long.

CHARMIAN
Like her! O Isis! 'tis impossible.

CLEOPATRA
I think so, Charmian: dull of tongue, and dwarfish!
What majesty is in her gait? Remember,
If e'er thou look'dst on majesty.

Messenger
She creeps:
Her motion and her station are as one;
She shows a body rather than a life,
A statue than a breather.

CLEOPATRA
Is this certain?

Messenger

Or I have no observance.

CHARMIAN
Three in Egypt
Cannot make better note.

CLEOPATRA
He's very knowing;
I do perceive't: there's nothing in her yet:
The fellow has good judgment.

CHARMIAN
Excellent.

CLEOPATRA
Guess at her years, I prithee.

Messenger
Madam,
She was a widow,--

CLEOPATRA
Widow! Charmian, hark.

Messenger
And I do think she's thirty.

CLEOPATRA
Bear'st thou her face in mind? is't long or round?

Messenger
Round even to faultiness.

CLEOPATRA
For the most part, too, they are foolish that are so.
Her hair, what colour?

Messenger
Brown, madam: and her forehead

As low as she would wish it.

CLEOPATRA
There's gold for thee.
Thou must not take my former sharpness ill:
I will employ thee back again; I find thee
Most fit for business: go make thee ready;
Our letters are prepared.

Exit Messenger

CHARMIAN
A proper man.

CLEOPATRA
Indeed, he is so: I repent me much
That so I harried him. Why, methinks, by him,
This creature's no such thing.

CHARMIAN
Nothing, madam.

CLEOPATRA
The man hath seen some majesty, and should know.

CHARMIAN
Hath he seen majesty? Isis else defend,
And serving you so long!

CLEOPATRA
I have one thing more to ask him yet, good Charmian:
But 'tis no matter; thou shalt bring him to me
Where I will write. All may be well enough.

CHARMIAN
I warrant you, madam.

Exeunt

SCENE IV. Athens. A room in MARK ANTONY's house.

Enter MARK ANTONY and OCTAVIA

MARK ANTONY
Nay, nay, Octavia, not only that,--
That were excusable, that, and thousands more
Of semblable import,--but he hath waged
New wars 'gainst Pompey; made his will, and read it
To public ear:
Spoke scantly of me: when perforce he could not
But pay me terms of honour, cold and sickly
He vented them; most narrow measure lent me:
When the best hint was given him, he not took't,
Or did it from his teeth.

OCTAVIA
O my good lord,
Believe not all; or, if you must believe,
Stomach not all. A more unhappy lady,
If this division chance, ne'er stood between,
Praying for both parts:
The good gods me presently,
When I shall pray, 'O bless my lord and husband!'
Undo that prayer, by crying out as loud,
'O, bless my brother!' Husband win, win brother,
Prays, and destroys the prayer; no midway
'Twixt these extremes at all.

MARK ANTONY
Gentle Octavia,
Let your best love draw to that point, which seeks
Best to preserve it: if I lose mine honour,
I lose myself: better I were not yours
Than yours so branchless. But, as you requested,
Yourself shall go between 's: the mean time, lady,
I'll raise the preparation of a war

Shall stain your brother: make your soonest haste;
So your desires are yours.

OCTAVIA
Thanks to my lord.
The Jove of power make me most weak, most weak,
Your reconciler! Wars 'twixt you twain would be
As if the world should cleave, and that slain men
Should solder up the rift.

MARK ANTONY
When it appears to you where this begins,
Turn your displeasure that way: for our faults
Can never be so equal, that your love
Can equally move with them. Provide your going;
Choose your own company, and command what cost
Your heart has mind to.

Exeunt

SCENE V. The same. Another room.

Enter DOMITIUS ENOBARBUS and EROS, meeting

DOMITIUS ENOBARBUS
How now, friend Eros!

EROS
There's strange news come, sir.

DOMITIUS ENOBARBUS
What, man?

EROS
Caesar and Lepidus have made wars upon Pompey.

DOMITIUS ENOBARBUS
This is old: what is the success?

EROS
Caesar, having made use of him in the wars 'gainst
Pompey, presently denied him rivality; would not let
him partake in the glory of the action: and not
resting here, accuses him of letters he had formerly
wrote to Pompey; upon his own appeal, seizes him: so
the poor third is up, till death enlarge his confine.

DOMITIUS ENOBARBUS
Then, world, thou hast a pair of chaps, no more;
And throw between them all the food thou hast,
They'll grind the one the other. Where's Antony?

EROS
He's walking in the garden--thus; and spurns
The rush that lies before him; cries, 'Fool Lepidus!'
And threats the throat of that his officer
That murder'd Pompey.

DOMITIUS ENOBARBUS
Our great navy's rigg'd.

EROS
For Italy and Caesar. More, Domitius;
My lord desires you presently: my news
I might have told hereafter.

DOMITIUS ENOBARBUS
'Twill be naught:
But let it be. Bring me to Antony.

EROS
Come, sir.

Exeunt

SCENE VI. Rome. OCTAVIUS CAESAR's house.

Enter OCTAVIUS CAESAR, AGRIPPA, and MECAENAS

OCTAVIUS CAESAR
Contemning Rome, he has done all this, and more,
In Alexandria: here's the manner of 't:
I' the market-place, on a tribunal silver'd,
Cleopatra and himself in chairs of gold
Were publicly enthroned: at the feet sat
Caesarion, whom they call my father's son,
And all the unlawful issue that their lust
Since then hath made between them. Unto her
He gave the stablishment of Egypt; made her
Of lower Syria, Cyprus, Lydia,
Absolute queen.

MECAENAS
This in the public eye?

OCTAVIUS CAESAR
I' the common show-place, where they exercise.
His sons he there proclaim'd the kings of kings:
Great Media, Parthia, and Armenia.
He gave to Alexander; to Ptolemy he assign'd
Syria, Cilicia, and Phoenicia: she
In the habiliments of the goddess Isis
That day appear'd; and oft before gave audience,
As 'tis reported, so.

MECAENAS
Let Rome be thus Inform'd.

AGRIPPA
Who, queasy with his insolence
Already, will their good thoughts call from him.

OCTAVIUS CAESAR
The people know it; and have now received
His accusations.

AGRIPPA
Who does he accuse?

OCTAVIUS CAESAR
Caesar: and that, having in Sicily
Sextus Pompeius spoil'd, we had not rated him
His part o' the isle: then does he say, he lent me
Some shipping unrestored: lastly, he frets
That Lepidus of the triumvirate
Should be deposed; and, being, that we detain
All his revenue.

AGRIPPA
Sir, this should be answer'd.

OCTAVIUS CAESAR
'Tis done already, and the messenger gone.
I have told him, Lepidus was grown too cruel;
That he his high authority abused,
And did deserve his change: for what I have conquer'd,
I grant him part; but then, in his Armenia,
And other of his conquer'd kingdoms, I
Demand the like.

MECAENAS
He'll never yield to that.

OCTAVIUS CAESAR
Nor must not then be yielded to in this.

Enter OCTAVIA with her train

OCTAVIA
Hail, Caesar, and my lord! hail, most dear Caesar!

OCTAVIUS CAESAR
That ever I should call thee castaway!

OCTAVIA
You have not call'd me so, nor have you cause.

OCTAVIUS CAESAR
Why have you stol'n upon us thus! You come not
Like Caesar's sister: the wife of Antony
Should have an army for an usher, and
The neighs of horse to tell of her approach
Long ere she did appear; the trees by the way
Should have borne men; and expectation fainted,
Longing for what it had not; nay, the dust
Should have ascended to the roof of heaven,
Raised by your populous troops: but you are come
A market-maid to Rome; and have prevented
The ostentation of our love, which, left unshown,
Is often left unloved; we should have met you
By sea and land; supplying every stage
With an augmented greeting.

OCTAVIA
Good my lord,
To come thus was I not constrain'd, but did
On my free will. My lord, Mark Antony,
Hearing that you prepared for war, acquainted
My grieved ear withal; whereon, I begg'd
His pardon for return.

OCTAVIUS CAESAR
Which soon he granted,
Being an obstruct 'tween his lust and him.

OCTAVIA
Do not say so, my lord.

OCTAVIUS CAESAR
I have eyes upon him,

And his affairs come to me on the wind.
Where is he now?

OCTAVIA
My lord, in Athens.

OCTAVIUS CAESAR
No, my most wronged sister; Cleopatra
Hath nodded him to her. He hath given his empire
Up to a whore; who now are levying
The kings o' the earth for war; he hath assembled
Bocchus, the king of Libya; Archelaus,
Of Cappadocia; Philadelphos, king
Of Paphlagonia; the Thracian king, Adallas;
King Malchus of Arabia; King of Pont;
Herod of Jewry; Mithridates, king
Of Comagene; Polemon and Amyntas,
The kings of Mede and Lycaonia,
With a more larger list of sceptres.

OCTAVIA
Ay me, most wretched,
That have my heart parted betwixt two friends
That do afflict each other!

OCTAVIUS CAESAR
Welcome hither:
Your letters did withhold our breaking forth;
Till we perceived, both how you were wrong led,
And we in negligent danger. Cheer your heart;
Be you not troubled with the time, which drives
O'er your content these strong necessities;
But let determined things to destiny
Hold unbewail'd their way. Welcome to Rome;
Nothing more dear to me. You are abused
Beyond the mark of thought: and the high gods,
To do you justice, make them ministers
Of us and those that love you. Best of comfort;
And ever welcome to us.

AGRIPPA
Welcome, lady.

MECAENAS
Welcome, dear madam.
Each heart in Rome does love and pity you:
Only the adulterous Antony, most large
In his abominations, turns you off;
And gives his potent regiment to a trull,
That noises it against us.

OCTAVIA
Is it so, sir?

OCTAVIUS CAESAR
Most certain. Sister, welcome: pray you,
Be ever known to patience: my dear'st sister!

Exeunt

SCENE VII. Near Actium. MARK ANTONY's camp.

Enter CLEOPATRA and DOMITIUS ENOBARBUS

CLEOPATRA
I will be even with thee, doubt it not.

DOMITIUS ENOBARBUS
But why, why, why?

CLEOPATRA
Thou hast forspoke my being in these wars,
And say'st it is not fit.

DOMITIUS ENOBARBUS
Well, is it, is it?

CLEOPATRA
If not denounced against us, why should not we
Be there in person?

DOMITIUS ENOBARBUS
[Aside] Well, I could reply:
If we should serve with horse and mares together,
The horse were merely lost; the mares would bear
A soldier and his horse.

CLEOPATRA
What is't you say?

DOMITIUS ENOBARBUS
Your presence needs must puzzle Antony;
Take from his heart, take from his brain,
from's time,
What should not then be spared. He is already
Traduced for levity; and 'tis said in Rome
That Photinus an eunuch and your maids
Manage this war.

CLEOPATRA
Sink Rome, and their tongues rot
That speak against us! A charge we bear i' the war,
And, as the president of my kingdom, will
Appear there for a man. Speak not against it:
I will not stay behind.

DOMITIUS ENOBARBUS
Nay, I have done.
Here comes the emperor.

Enter MARK ANTONY and CANIDIUS

MARK ANTONY
Is it not strange, Canidius,
That from Tarentum and Brundusium
He could so quickly cut the Ionian sea,
And take in Toryne? You have heard on't, sweet?

CLEOPATRA
Celerity is never more admired
Than by the negligent.

MARK ANTONY
A good rebuke,
Which might have well becomed the best of men,
To taunt at slackness. Canidius, we
Will fight with him by sea.

CLEOPATRA
By sea! what else?

CANIDIUS
Why will my lord do so?

MARK ANTONY
For that he dares us to't.

DOMITIUS ENOBARBUS
So hath my lord dared him to single fight.

CANIDIUS
Ay, and to wage this battle at Pharsalia.
Where Caesar fought with Pompey: but these offers,
Which serve not for his vantage, be shakes off;
And so should you.

DOMITIUS ENOBARBUS
Your ships are not well mann'd;
Your mariners are muleters, reapers, people
Ingross'd by swift impress; in Caesar's fleet
Are those that often have 'gainst Pompey fought:
Their ships are yare; yours, heavy: no disgrace
Shall fall you for refusing him at sea,
Being prepared for land.

MARK ANTONY
By sea, by sea.

DOMITIUS ENOBARBUS
Most worthy sir, you therein throw away
The absolute soldiership you have by land;
Distract your army, which doth most consist
Of war-mark'd footmen; leave unexecuted
Your own renowned knowledge; quite forego
The way which promises assurance; and
Give up yourself merely to chance and hazard,
From firm security.

MARK ANTONY
I'll fight at sea.

CLEOPATRA
I have sixty sails, Caesar none better.

MARK ANTONY
Our overplus of shipping will we burn;

And, with the rest full-mann'd, from the head of
Actium
Beat the approaching Caesar. But if we fail,
We then can do't at land.

Enter a Messenger

Thy business?

Messenger
The news is true, my lord; he is descried;
Caesar has taken Toryne.

MARK ANTONY
Can he be there in person? 'tis impossible;
Strange that power should be. Canidius,
Our nineteen legions thou shalt hold by land,
And our twelve thousand horse. We'll to our ship:
Away, my Thetis!

Enter a Soldier

How now, worthy soldier?

Soldier
O noble emperor, do not fight by sea;
Trust not to rotten planks: do you misdoubt
This sword and these my wounds? Let the Egyptians
And the Phoenicians go a-ducking; we
Have used to conquer, standing on the earth,
And fighting foot to foot.

MARK ANTONY
Well, well: away!

Exeunt MARK ANTONY, QUEEN CLEOPATRA, and
DOMITIUS ENOBARBUS

Soldier
By Hercules, I think I am i' the right.

CANIDIUS
Soldier, thou art: but his whole action grows
Not in the power on't: so our leader's led,
And we are women's men.

Soldier
You keep by land
The legions and the horse whole, do you not?

CANIDIUS
Marcus Octavius, Marcus Justeius,
Publicola, and Caelius, are for sea:
But we keep whole by land. This speed of Caesar's
Carries beyond belief.

Soldier
While he was yet in Rome,
His power went out in such distractions as
Beguiled all spies.

CANIDIUS
Who's his lieutenant, hear you?

Soldier
They say, one Taurus.

CANIDIUS
Well I know the man.

Enter a Messenger

Messenger
The emperor calls Canidius.

CANIDIUS
With news the time's with labour, and throes forth,

Each minute, some.

Exeunt

SCENE VIII. A plain near Actium.

Enter OCTAVIUS CAESAR, and TAURUS, with his
army, marching

OCTAVIUS CAESAR
Taurus!

TAURUS
My lord?

OCTAVIUS CAESAR
Strike not by land; keep whole: provoke not battle,
Till we have done at sea. Do not exceed
The prescript of this scroll: our fortune lies
Upon this jump.

Exeunt

SCENE IX. Another part of the plain.

Enter MARK ANTONY and DOMITIUS ENOBARBUS

MARK ANTONY
Set we our squadrons on yond side o' the hill,
In eye of Caesar's battle; from which place
We may the number of the ships behold,
And so proceed accordingly.

Exeunt

SCENE X. Another part of the plain.

CANIDIUS marcheth with his land army one way over the stage; and TAURUS, the lieutenant of OCTAVIUS CAESAR, the other way. After their going in, is heard the noise of a sea-fight

Alarum. Enter DOMITIUS ENOBARBUS

DOMITIUS ENOBARBUS
Naught, naught all, naught! I can behold no longer:
The Antoniad, the Egyptian admiral,
With all their sixty, fly and turn the rudder:
To see't mine eyes are blasted.

Enter SCARUS

SCARUS
Gods and goddesses,
All the whole synod of them!

DOMITIUS ENOBARBUS
What's thy passion!

SCARUS
The greater cantle of the world is lost
With very ignorance; we have kiss'd away
Kingdoms and provinces.

DOMITIUS ENOBARBUS
How appears the fight?

SCARUS
On our side like the token'd pestilence,
Where death is sure. Yon ribaudred nag of Egypt,--
Whom leprosy o'ertake!--i' the midst o' the fight,
When vantage like a pair of twins appear'd,
Both as the same, or rather ours the elder,

The breese upon her, like a cow in June,
Hoists sails and flies.

DOMITIUS ENOBARBUS
That I beheld:
Mine eyes did sicken at the sight, and could not
Endure a further view.

SCARUS
She once being loof'd,
The noble ruin of her magic, Antony,
Claps on his sea-wing, and, like a doting mallard,
Leaving the fight in height, flies after her:
I never saw an action of such shame;
Experience, manhood, honour, ne'er before
Did violate so itself.

DOMITIUS ENOBARBUS
Alack, alack!

Enter CANIDIUS

CANIDIUS
Our fortune on the sea is out of breath,
And sinks most lamentably. Had our general
Been what he knew himself, it had gone well:
O, he has given example for our flight,
Most grossly, by his own!

DOMITIUS ENOBARBUS
Ay, are you thereabouts?
Why, then, good night indeed.

CANIDIUS
Toward Peloponnesus are they fled.

SCARUS
'Tis easy to't; and there I will attend
What further comes.

CANIDIUS
To Caesar will I render
My legions and my horse: six kings already
Show me the way of yielding.

DOMITIUS ENOBARBUS
I'll yet follow
The wounded chance of Antony, though my reason
Sits in the wind against me.

Exeunt

SCENE XI. Alexandria. CLEOPATRA's palace.

Enter MARK ANTONY with Attendants

MARK ANTONY
Hark! the land bids me tread no more upon't;
It is ashamed to bear me! Friends, come hither:
I am so lated in the world, that I
Have lost my way for ever: I have a ship
Laden with gold; take that, divide it; fly,
And make your peace with Caesar.

All
Fly! not we.

MARK ANTONY
I have fled myself; and have instructed cowards
To run and show their shoulders. Friends, be gone;
I have myself resolved upon a course
Which has no need of you; be gone:
My treasure's in the harbour, take it. O,
I follow'd that I blush to look upon:
My very hairs do mutiny; for the white
Reprove the brown for rashness, and they them
For fear and doting. Friends, be gone: you shall
Have letters from me to some friends that will
Sweep your way for you. Pray you, look not sad,
Nor make replies of loathness: take the hint
Which my despair proclaims; let that be left
Which leaves itself: to the sea-side straightway:
I will possess you of that ship and treasure.
Leave me, I pray, a little: pray you now:
Nay, do so; for, indeed, I have lost command,
Therefore I pray you: I'll see you by and by.

Sits down

Enter CLEOPATRA led by CHARMIAN and IRAS;
EROS following

EROS
Nay, gentle madam, to him, comfort him.

IRAS
Do, most dear queen.

CHARMIAN
Do! why: what else?

CLEOPATRA
Let me sit down. O Juno!

MARK ANTONY
No, no, no, no, no.

EROS
See you here, sir?

MARK ANTONY
O fie, fie, fie!

CHARMIAN
Madam!

IRAS
Madam, O good empress!

EROS
Sir, sir,--

MARK ANTONY
Yes, my lord, yes; he at Philippi kept
His sword e'en like a dancer; while I struck
The lean and wrinkled Cassius; and 'twas I
That the mad Brutus ended: he alone
Dealt on lieutenantry, and no practise had

In the brave squares of war: yet now--No matter.

CLEOPATRA
Ah, stand by.

EROS
The queen, my lord, the queen.

IRAS
Go to him, madam, speak to him:
He is unqualitied with very shame.

CLEOPATRA
Well then, sustain him: O!

EROS
Most noble sir, arise; the queen approaches:
Her head's declined, and death will seize her, but
Your comfort makes the rescue.

MARK ANTONY
I have offended reputation,
A most unnoble swerving.

EROS
Sir, the queen.

MARK ANTONY
O, whither hast thou led me, Egypt? See,
How I convey my shame out of thine eyes
By looking back what I have left behind
'Stroy'd in dishonour.

CLEOPATRA
O my lord, my lord,
Forgive my fearful sails! I little thought
You would have follow'd.

MARK ANTONY
Egypt, thou knew'st too well
My heart was to thy rudder tied by the strings,
And thou shouldst tow me after: o'er my spirit
Thy full supremacy thou knew'st, and that
Thy beck might from the bidding of the gods
Command me.

CLEOPATRA
O, my pardon!

MARK ANTONY
Now I must
To the young man send humble treaties, dodge
And palter in the shifts of lowness; who
With half the bulk o' the world play'd as I pleased,
Making and marring fortunes. You did know
How much you were my conqueror; and that
My sword, made weak by my affection, would
Obey it on all cause.

CLEOPATRA
Pardon, pardon!

MARK ANTONY
Fall not a tear, I say; one of them rates
All that is won and lost: give me a kiss;
Even this repays me. We sent our schoolmaster;
Is he come back? Love, I am full of lead.
Some wine, within there, and our viands! Fortune
knows
We scorn her most when most she offers blows.

Exeunt

SCENE XII. Egypt. OCTAVIUS CAESAR's camp.

Enter OCTAVIUS CAESAR, DOLABELLA, THYREUS, with others

OCTAVIUS CAESAR
Let him appear that's come from Antony.
Know you him?

DOLABELLA
Caesar, 'tis his schoolmaster:
An argument that he is pluck'd, when hither
He sends so poor a pinion off his wing,
Which had superfluous kings for messengers
Not many moons gone by.

Enter EUPHRONIUS, ambassador from MARK
ANTONY

OCTAVIUS CAESAR
Approach, and speak.

EUPHRONIUS
Such as I am, I come from Antony:
I was of late as petty to his ends
As is the morn-dew on the myrtle-leaf
To his grand sea.

OCTAVIUS CAESAR
Be't so: declare thine office.

EUPHRONIUS
Lord of his fortunes he salutes thee, and
Requires to live in Egypt: which not granted,
He lessens his requests; and to thee sues
To let him breathe between the heavens and earth,
A private man in Athens: this for him.

Next, Cleopatra does confess thy greatness;
Submits her to thy might; and of thee craves
The circle of the Ptolemies for her heirs,
Now hazarded to thy grace.

OCTAVIUS CAESAR
For Antony,
I have no ears to his request. The queen
Of audience nor desire shall fail, so she
From Egypt drive her all-disgraced friend,
Or take his life there: this if she perform,
She shall not sue unheard. So to them both.

EUPHRONIUS
Fortune pursue thee!

OCTAVIUS CAESAR
Bring him through the bands.

Exit EUPHRONIUS

To THYREUS

From Antony win Cleopatra: promise,
And in our name, what she requires; add more,
From thine invention, offers: women are not
In their best fortunes strong; but want will perjure
The ne'er touch'd vestal: try thy cunning, Thyreus;
Make thine own edict for thy pains, which we
Will answer as a law.

THYREUS
Caesar, I go.

OCTAVIUS CAESAR
Observe how Antony becomes his flaw,
And what thou think'st his very action speaks
In every power that moves.

THYREUS
Caesar, I shall.

Exeunt

SCENE XIII. Alexandria. CLEOPATRA's palace.

Enter CLEOPATRA, DOMITIUS ENOBARBUS,
CHARMIAN, and IRAS

CLEOPATRA
What shall we do, Enobarbus?

DOMITIUS ENOBARBUS
Think, and die.

CLEOPATRA
Is Antony or we in fault for this?

DOMITIUS ENOBARBUS
Antony only, that would make his will
Lord of his reason. What though you fled
From that great face of war, whose several ranges
Frighted each other? why should he follow?
The itch of his affection should not then
Have nick'd his captainship; at such a point,
When half to half the world opposed, he being
The meered question: 'twas a shame no less
Than was his loss, to course your flying flags,
And leave his navy gazing.

CLEOPATRA
Prithee, peace.

Enter MARK ANTONY with EUPHRONIUS, the
Ambassador

MARK ANTONY
Is that his answer?

EUPHRONIUS
Ay, my lord.

MARK ANTONY
The queen shall then have courtesy, so she
Will yield us up.

EUPHRONIUS
He says so.

MARK ANTONY
Let her know't.
To the boy Caesar send this grizzled head,
And he will fill thy wishes to the brim
With principalities.

CLEOPATRA
That head, my lord?

MARK ANTONY
To him again: tell him he wears the rose
Of youth upon him; from which the world should note
Something particular: his coin, ships, legions,
May be a coward's; whose ministers would prevail
Under the service of a child as soon
As i' the command of Caesar: I dare him therefore
To lay his gay comparisons apart,
And answer me declined, sword against sword,
Ourselves alone. I'll write it: follow me.

Exeunt MARK ANTONY and EUPHRONIUS

DOMITIUS ENOBARBUS
[Aside] Yes, like enough, high-battled Caesar will
Unstate his happiness, and be staged to the show,
Against a sworder! I see men's judgments are
A parcel of their fortunes; and things outward
Do draw the inward quality after them,
To suffer all alike. That he should dream,
Knowing all measures, the full Caesar will
Answer his emptiness! Caesar, thou hast subdued
His judgment too.

Enter an Attendant

Attendant
A messenger from CAESAR.

CLEOPATRA
What, no more ceremony? See, my women!
Against the blown rose may they stop their nose
That kneel'd unto the buds. Admit him, sir.

Exit Attendant

DOMITIUS ENOBARBUS
[Aside] Mine honesty and I begin to square.
The loyalty well held to fools does make
Our faith mere folly: yet he that can endure
To follow with allegiance a fall'n lord
Does conquer him that did his master conquer
And earns a place i' the story.

Enter THYREUS

CLEOPATRA
Caesar's will?

THYREUS
Hear it apart.

CLEOPATRA
None but friends: say boldly.

THYREUS
So, haply, are they friends to Antony.

DOMITIUS ENOBARBUS
He needs as many, sir, as Caesar has;
Or needs not us. If Caesar please, our master
Will leap to be his friend: for us, you know,

Whose he is we are, and that is, Caesar's.

THYREUS
So.
Thus then, thou most renown'd: Caesar entreats,
Not to consider in what case thou stand'st,
Further than he is Caesar.

CLEOPATRA
Go on: right royal.

THYREUS
He knows that you embrace not Antony
As you did love, but as you fear'd him.

CLEOPATRA
O!

THYREUS
The scars upon your honour, therefore, he
Does pity, as constrained blemishes,
Not as deserved.

CLEOPATRA
He is a god, and knows
What is most right: mine honour was not yielded,
But conquer'd merely.

DOMITIUS ENOBARBUS
[Aside] To be sure of that,
I will ask Antony. Sir, sir, thou art so leaky,
That we must leave thee to thy sinking, for
Thy dearest quit thee.

Exit

THYREUS
Shall I say to Caesar
What you require of him? for he partly begs

To be desired to give. It much would please him,
That of his fortunes you should make a staff
To lean upon: but it would warm his spirits,
To hear from me you had left Antony,
And put yourself under his shrowd,
The universal landlord.

CLEOPATRA
What's your name?

THYREUS
My name is Thyreus.

CLEOPATRA
Most kind messenger,
Say to great Caesar this: in deputation
I kiss his conquering hand: tell him, I am prompt
To lay my crown at 's feet, and there to kneel:
Tell him from his all-obeying breath I hear
The doom of Egypt.

THYREUS
'Tis your noblest course.
Wisdom and fortune combating together,
If that the former dare but what it can,
No chance may shake it. Give me grace to lay
My duty on your hand.

CLEOPATRA
Your Caesar's father oft,
When he hath mused of taking kingdoms in,
Bestow'd his lips on that unworthy place,
As it rain'd kisses.

Re-enter MARK ANTONY and DOMITIUS ENOBARBUS

MARK ANTONY
Favours, by Jove that thunders!
What art thou, fellow?

THYREUS
One that but performs
The bidding of the fullest man, and worthiest
To have command obey'd.

DOMITIUS ENOBARBUS
[Aside] You will be whipp'd.

MARK ANTONY
Approach, there! Ah, you kite! Now, gods
and devils!
Authority melts from me: of late, when I cried 'Ho!'
Like boys unto a muss, kings would start forth,
And cry 'Your will?' Have you no ears? I am
Antony yet.

Enter Attendants

Take hence this Jack, and whip him.

DOMITIUS ENOBARBUS
[Aside] 'Tis better playing with a lion's whelp
Than with an old one dying.

MARK ANTONY
Moon and stars!
Whip him. Were't twenty of the greatest tributaries
That do acknowledge Caesar, should I find them
So saucy with the hand of she here,--what's her name,
Since she was Cleopatra? Whip him, fellows,
Till, like a boy, you see him cringe his face,
And whine aloud for mercy: take him hence.

THYREUS
Mark Antony!

MARK ANTONY
Tug him away: being whipp'd,

Bring him again: this Jack of Caesar's shall
Bear us an errand to him.

Exeunt Attendants with THYREUS

You were half blasted ere I knew you: ha!
Have I my pillow left unpress'd in Rome,
Forborne the getting of a lawful race,
And by a gem of women, to be abused
By one that looks on feeders?

CLEOPATRA
Good my lord,--

MARK ANTONY
You have been a boggler ever:
But when we in our viciousness grow hard--
O misery on't!--the wise gods seel our eyes;
In our own filth drop our clear judgments; make us
Adore our errors; laugh at's, while we strut
To our confusion.

CLEOPATRA
O, is't come to this?

MARK ANTONY
I found you as a morsel cold upon
Dead Caesar's trencher; nay, you were a fragment
Of Cneius Pompey's; besides what hotter hours,
Unregister'd in vulgar fame, you have
Luxuriously pick'd out: for, I am sure,
Though you can guess what temperance should be,
You know not what it is.

CLEOPATRA
Wherefore is this?

MARK ANTONY
To let a fellow that will take rewards

And say 'God quit you!' be familiar with
My playfellow, your hand; this kingly seal
And plighter of high hearts! O, that I were
Upon the hill of Basan, to outroar
The horned herd! for I have savage cause;
And to proclaim it civilly, were like
A halter'd neck which does the hangman thank
For being yare about him.

Re-enter Attendants with THYREUS

Is he whipp'd?

First Attendant
Soundly, my lord.

MARK ANTONY
Cried he? and begg'd a' pardon?

First Attendant
He did ask favour.

MARK ANTONY
If that thy father live, let him repent
Thou wast not made his daughter; and be thou sorry
To follow Caesar in his triumph, since
Thou hast been whipp'd for following him: henceforth
The white hand of a lady fever thee,
Shake thou to look on 't. Get thee back to Caesar,
Tell him thy entertainment: look, thou say
He makes me angry with him; for he seems
Proud and disdainful, harping on what I am,
Not what he knew I was: he makes me angry;
And at this time most easy 'tis to do't,
When my good stars, that were my former guides,
Have empty left their orbs, and shot their fires
Into the abysm of hell. If he mislike
My speech and what is done, tell him he has
Hipparchus, my enfranched bondman, whom

He may at pleasure whip, or hang, or torture,
As he shall like, to quit me: urge it thou:
Hence with thy stripes, begone!

Exit THYREUS

CLEOPATRA
Have you done yet?

MARK ANTONY
Alack, our terrene moon
Is now eclipsed; and it portends alone
The fall of Antony!

CLEOPATRA
I must stay his time.

MARK ANTONY
To flatter Caesar, would you mingle eyes
With one that ties his points?

CLEOPATRA
Not know me yet?

MARK ANTONY
Cold-hearted toward me?

CLEOPATRA
Ah, dear, if I be so,
From my cold heart let heaven engender hail,
And poison it in the source; and the first stone
Drop in my neck: as it determines, so
Dissolve my life! The next Caesarion smite!
Till by degrees the memory of my womb,
Together with my brave Egyptians all,
By the discandying of this pelleted storm,
Lie graveless, till the flies and gnats of Nile
Have buried them for prey!

MARK ANTONY
I am satisfied.
Caesar sits down in Alexandria; where
I will oppose his fate. Our force by land
Hath nobly held; our sever'd navy too
Have knit again, and fleet, threatening most sea-like.
Where hast thou been, my heart? Dost thou hear,
lady?
If from the field I shall return once more
To kiss these lips, I will appear in blood;
I and my sword will earn our chronicle:
There's hope in't yet.

CLEOPATRA
That's my brave lord!

MARK ANTONY
I will be treble-sinew'd, hearted, breathed,
And fight maliciously: for when mine hours
Were nice and lucky, men did ransom lives
Of me for jests; but now I'll set my teeth,
And send to darkness all that stop me. Come,
Let's have one other gaudy night: call to me
All my sad captains; fill our bowls once more;
Let's mock the midnight bell.

CLEOPATRA
It is my birth-day:
I had thought to have held it poor: but, since my lord
Is Antony again, I will be Cleopatra.

MARK ANTONY
We will yet do well.

CLEOPATRA
Call all his noble captains to my lord.

MARK ANTONY
Do so, we'll speak to them; and to-night I'll force

The wine peep through their scars. Come on, my
queen;
There's sap in't yet. The next time I do fight,
I'll make death love me; for I will contend
Even with his pestilent scythe.

Exeunt all but DOMITIUS ENOBARBUS

DOMITIUS ENOBARBUS
Now he'll outstare the lightning. To be furious,
Is to be frighted out of fear; and in that mood
The dove will peck the estridge; and I see still,
A diminution in our captain's brain
Restores his heart: when valour preys on reason,
It eats the sword it fights with. I will seek
Some way to leave him.

Exit

ACT IV

SCENE I. Before Alexandria. OCTAVIUS CAESAR's camp.

Enter OCTAVIUS CAESAR, AGRIPPA, and
MECAENAS, with his Army; OCTAVIUS CAESAR
reading a letter

OCTAVIUS CAESAR
He calls me boy; and chides, as he had power
To beat me out of Egypt; my messenger
He hath whipp'd with rods; dares me to personal
combat,
Caesar to Antony: let the old ruffian know
I have many other ways to die; meantime
Laugh at his challenge.

MECAENAS
Caesar must think,
When one so great begins to rage, he's hunted
Even to falling. Give him no breath, but now
Make boot of his distraction: never anger
Made good guard for itself.

OCTAVIUS CAESAR
Let our best heads
Know, that to-morrow the last of many battles
We mean to fight: within our files there are,
Of those that served Mark Antony but late,
Enough to fetch him in. See it done:
And feast the army; we have store to do't,
And they have earn'd the waste. Poor Antony!

Exeunt

SCENE II. Alexandria. CLEOPATRA's palace.

Enter MARK ANTONY, CLEOPATRA, DOMITIUS
ENOBARBUS, CHARMIAN, IRAS, ALEXAS, with others

MARK ANTONY
He will not fight with me, Domitius.

DOMITIUS ENOBARBUS
No.

MARK ANTONY
Why should he not?

DOMITIUS ENOBARBUS
He thinks, being twenty times of better fortune,
He is twenty men to one.

MARK ANTONY
To-morrow, soldier,
By sea and land I'll fight: or I will live,
Or bathe my dying honour in the blood
Shall make it live again. Woo't thou fight well?

DOMITIUS ENOBARBUS
I'll strike, and cry 'Take all.'

MARK ANTONY
Well said; come on.
Call forth my household servants: let's to-night
Be bounteous at our meal.

Enter three or four Servitors

Give me thy hand,
Thou hast been rightly honest;--so hast thou;--
Thou,--and thou,--and thou:--you have served me
well,

And kings have been your fellows.

CLEOPATRA
[Aside to DOMITIUS ENOBARBUS] What means this?

DOMITIUS ENOBARBUS
[Aside to CLEOPATRA] 'Tis one of those odd
tricks which sorrow shoots
Out of the mind.

MARK ANTONY
And thou art honest too.
I wish I could be made so many men,
And all of you clapp'd up together in
An Antony, that I might do you service
So good as you have done.

All
The gods forbid!

MARK ANTONY
Well, my good fellows, wait on me to-night:
Scant not my cups; and make as much of me
As when mine empire was your fellow too,
And suffer'd my command.

CLEOPATRA
[Aside to DOMITIUS ENOBARBUS] What does he
mean?

DOMITIUS ENOBARBUS
[Aside to CLEOPATRA] To make his followers weep.

MARK ANTONY
Tend me to-night;
May be it is the period of your duty:
Haply you shall not see me more; or if,
A mangled shadow: perchance to-morrow
You'll serve another master. I look on you

As one that takes his leave. Mine honest friends,
I turn you not away; but, like a master
Married to your good service, stay till death:
Tend me to-night two hours, I ask no more,
And the gods yield you for't!

DOMITIUS ENOBARBUS
What mean you, sir,
To give them this discomfort? Look, they weep;
And I, an ass, am onion-eyed: for shame,
Transform us not to women.

MARK ANTONY
Ho, ho, ho!
Now the witch take me, if I meant it thus!
Grace grow where those drops fall!
My hearty friends,
You take me in too dolorous a sense;
For I spake to you for your comfort; did desire you
To burn this night with torches: know, my hearts,
I hope well of to-morrow; and will lead you
Where rather I'll expect victorious life
Than death and honour. Let's to supper, come,
And drown consideration.

Exeunt

.

SCENE III. The same. Before the palace.

Enter two Soldiers to their guard

First Soldier
Brother, good night: to-morrow is the day.

Second Soldier
It will determine one way: fare you well.
Heard you of nothing strange about the streets?

First Soldier
Nothing. What news?

Second Soldier
Belike 'tis but a rumour. Good night to you.

First Soldier
Well, sir, good night.

Enter two other Soldiers

Second Soldier
Soldiers, have careful watch.

Third Soldier
And you. Good night, good night.

They place themselves in every corner of the stage

Fourth Soldier
Here we: and if to-morrow
Our navy thrive, I have an absolute hope
Our landmen will stand up.

Third Soldier
'Tis a brave army,
And full of purpose.

Music of the hautboys as under the stage

Fourth Soldier
Peace! what noise?

First Soldier
List, list!

Second Soldier
Hark!

First Soldier
Music i' the air.

Third Soldier
Under the earth.

Fourth Soldier
It signs well, does it not?

Third Soldier
No.

First Soldier
Peace, I say!
What should this mean?

Second Soldier
'Tis the god Hercules, whom Antony loved,
Now leaves him.

First Soldier
Walk; let's see if other watchmen
Do hear what we do?

They advance to another post

Second Soldier
How now, masters!

All
[Speaking together] How now!
How now! do you hear this?

First Soldier
Ay; is't not strange?

Third Soldier
Do you hear, masters? do you hear?

First Soldier
Follow the noise so far as we have quarter;
Let's see how it will give off.

All
Content. 'Tis strange.

Exeunt

SCENE IV. The same. A room in the palace.

Enter MARK ANTONY and CLEOPATRA, CHARMIAN,
and others attending

MARK ANTONY
Eros! mine armour, Eros!

CLEOPATRA
Sleep a little.

MARK ANTONY
No, my chuck. Eros, come; mine armour, Eros!

Enter EROS with armour

Come good fellow, put mine iron on:
If fortune be not ours to-day, it is
Because we brave her: come.

CLEOPATRA
Nay, I'll help too.
What's this for?

MARK ANTONY
Ah, let be, let be! thou art
The armourer of my heart: false, false; this, this.

CLEOPATRA
Sooth, la, I'll help: thus it must be.

MARK ANTONY
Well, well;
We shall thrive now. Seest thou, my good fellow?
Go put on thy defences.

EROS
Briefly, sir.

CLEOPATRA
Is not this buckled well?

MARK ANTONY
Rarely, rarely:
He that unbuckles this, till we do please
To daff't for our repose, shall hear a storm.
Thou fumblest, Eros; and my queen's a squire
More tight at this than thou: dispatch. O love,
That thou couldst see my wars to-day, and knew'st
The royal occupation! thou shouldst see
A workman in't.

Enter an armed Soldier

Good morrow to thee; welcome:
Thou look'st like him that knows a warlike charge:
To business that we love we rise betime,
And go to't with delight.

Soldier
A thousand, sir,
Early though't be, have on their riveted trim,
And at the port expect you.

Shout. Trumpets flourish

Enter Captains and Soldiers

Captain
The morn is fair. Good morrow, general.

All
Good morrow, general.

MARK ANTONY
'Tis well blown, lads:
This morning, like the spirit of a youth

That means to be of note, begins betimes.
So, so; come, give me that: this way; well said.
Fare thee well, dame, whate'er becomes of me:
This is a soldier's kiss: rebukeable

Kisses her

And worthy shameful cheque it were, to stand
On more mechanic compliment; I'll leave thee
Now, like a man of steel. You that will fight,
Follow me close; I'll bring you to't. Adieu.

Exeunt MARK ANTONY, EROS, Captains, and Soldiers

CHARMIAN
Please you, retire to your chamber.

CLEOPATRA
Lead me.
He goes forth gallantly. That he and Caesar might
Determine this great war in single fight!
Then Antony,--but now--Well, on.

Exeunt

SCENE V. Alexandria. MARK ANTONY's camp.

Trumpets sound. Enter MARK ANTONY and EROS; a Soldier meeting them

Soldier
The gods make this a happy day to Antony!

MARK ANTONY
Would thou and those thy scars had once prevail'd
To make me fight at land!

Soldier
Hadst thou done so,
The kings that have revolted, and the soldier
That has this morning left thee, would have still
Follow'd thy heels.

MARK ANTONY
Who's gone this morning?

Soldier
Who!
One ever near thee: call for Enobarbus,
He shall not hear thee; or from Caesar's camp
Say 'I am none of thine.'

MARK ANTONY
What say'st thou?

Soldier
Sir,
He is with Caesar.

EROS
Sir, his chests and treasure
He has not with him.

MARK ANTONY
Is he gone?

Soldier
Most certain.

MARK ANTONY
Go, Eros, send his treasure after; do it;
Detain no jot, I charge thee: write to him--
I will subscribe--gentle adieus and greetings;
Say that I wish he never find more cause
To change a master. O, my fortunes have
Corrupted honest men! Dispatch.--Enobarbus!

Exeunt

SCENE VI. Alexandria. OCTAVIUS CAESAR's camp.

Flourish. Enter OCTAVIUS CAESAR, AGRIPPA, with
DOMITIUS ENOBARBUS, and others

OCTAVIUS CAESAR
Go forth, Agrippa, and begin the fight:
Our will is Antony be took alive;
Make it so known.

AGRIPPA
Caesar, I shall.

Exit

OCTAVIUS CAESAR
The time of universal peace is near:
Prove this a prosperous day, the three-nook'd world
Shall bear the olive freely.

Enter a Messenger

Messenger
Antony
Is come into the field.

OCTAVIUS CAESAR
Go charge Agrippa
Plant those that have revolted in the van,
That Antony may seem to spend his fury
Upon himself.

Exeunt all but DOMITIUS ENOBARBUS

DOMITIUS ENOBARBUS
Alexas did revolt; and went to Jewry on
Affairs of Antony; there did persuade
Great Herod to incline himself to Caesar,
And leave his master Antony: for this pains
Caesar hath hang'd him. Canidius and the rest
That fell away have entertainment, but
No honourable trust. I have done ill;
Of which I do accuse myself so sorely,
That I will joy no more.

Enter a Soldier of CAESAR's

Soldier
Enobarbus, Antony
Hath after thee sent all thy treasure, with
His bounty overplus: the messenger
Came on my guard; and at thy tent is now
Unloading of his mules.

DOMITIUS ENOBARBUS
I give it you.

Soldier
Mock not, Enobarbus.
I tell you true: best you safed the bringer
Out of the host; I must attend mine office,
Or would have done't myself. Your emperor
Continues still a Jove.

Exit

DOMITIUS ENOBARBUS
I am alone the villain of the earth,
And feel I am so most. O Antony,
Thou mine of bounty, how wouldst thou have paid
My better service, when my turpitude
Thou dost so crown with gold! This blows my heart:
If swift thought break it not, a swifter mean

Shall outstrike thought: but thought will do't, I feel.
I fight against thee! No: I will go seek
Some ditch wherein to die; the foul'st best fits
My latter part of life.

Exit

SCENE VII. Field of battle between the camps.

Alarum. Drums and trumpets. Enter AGRIPPA and others

AGRIPPA
Retire, we have engaged ourselves too far:
Caesar himself has work, and our oppression
Exceeds what we expected.

Exeunt

Alarums. Enter MARK ANTONY and SCARUS
wounded

SCARUS
O my brave emperor, this is fought indeed!
Had we done so at first, we had droven them home
With clouts about their heads.

MARK ANTONY
Thou bleed'st apace.

SCARUS
I had a wound here that was like a T,
But now 'tis made an H.

MARK ANTONY
They do retire.

SCARUS
We'll beat 'em into bench-holes: I have yet
Room for six scotches more.

Enter EROS

EROS
They are beaten, sir, and our advantage serves

For a fair victory.

SCARUS
Let us score their backs,
And snatch 'em up, as we take hares, behind:
'Tis sport to maul a runner.

MARK ANTONY
I will reward thee
Once for thy spritely comfort, and ten-fold
For thy good valour. Come thee on.

SCARUS
I'll halt after.

Exeunt

SCENE VIII. Under the walls of Alexandria.

Alarum. Enter MARK ANTONY, in a march; SCARUS,
with others

MARK ANTONY
We have beat him to his camp: run one before,
And let the queen know of our gests. To-morrow,
Before the sun shall see 's, we'll spill the blood
That has to-day escaped. I thank you all;
For doughty-handed are you, and have fought
Not as you served the cause, but as 't had been
Each man's like mine; you have shown all Hectors.
Enter the city, clip your wives, your friends,
Tell them your feats; whilst they with joyful tears
Wash the congealment from your wounds, and kiss
The honour'd gashes whole.

To SCARUS

Give me thy hand

Enter CLEOPATRA, attended

To this great fairy I'll commend thy acts,
Make her thanks bless thee.

To CLEOPATRA

O thou day o' the world,
Chain mine arm'd neck; leap thou, attire and all,
Through proof of harness to my heart, and there
Ride on the pants triumphing!

CLEOPATRA
Lord of lords!
O infinite virtue, comest thou smiling from
The world's great snare uncaught?

MARK ANTONY
My nightingale,
We have beat them to their beds. What, girl!
though grey
Do something mingle with our younger brown, yet ha'
we
A brain that nourishes our nerves, and can
Get goal for goal of youth. Behold this man;
Commend unto his lips thy favouring hand:
Kiss it, my warrior: he hath fought to-day
As if a god, in hate of mankind, had
Destroy'd in such a shape.

CLEOPATRA
I'll give thee, friend,
An armour all of gold; it was a king's.

MARK ANTONY
He has deserved it, were it carbuncled
Like holy Phoebus' car. Give me thy hand:
Through Alexandria make a jolly march;
Bear our hack'd targets like the men that owe them:
Had our great palace the capacity
To camp this host, we all would sup together,
And drink carouses to the next day's fate,
Which promises royal peril. Trumpeters,
With brazen din blast you the city's ear;
Make mingle with rattling tabourines;
That heaven and earth may strike their sounds
together,
Applauding our approach.

Exeunt

SCENE IX. OCTAVIUS CAESAR's camp.

Sentinels at their post

First Soldier
If we be not relieved within this hour,
We must return to the court of guard: the night
Is shiny; and they say we shall embattle
By the second hour i' the morn.

Second Soldier
This last day was
A shrewd one to's.

Enter DOMITIUS ENOBARBUS

DOMITIUS ENOBARBUS
O, bear me witness, night,--

Third Soldier
What man is this?

Second Soldier
Stand close, and list him.

DOMITIUS ENOBARBUS
Be witness to me, O thou blessed moon,
When men revolted shall upon record
Bear hateful memory, poor Enobarbus did
Before thy face repent!

First Soldier
Enobarbus!

Third Soldier
Peace!
Hark further.

DOMITIUS ENOBARBUS
O sovereign mistress of true melancholy,
The poisonous damp of night disponge upon me,
That life, a very rebel to my will,
May hang no longer on me: throw my heart
Against the flint and hardness of my fault:
Which, being dried with grief, will break to powder,
And finish all foul thoughts. O Antony,
Nobler than my revolt is infamous,
Forgive me in thine own particular;
But let the world rank me in register
A master-leaver and a fugitive:
O Antony! O Antony!

Dies

Second Soldier
Let's speak To him.

First Soldier
Let's hear him, for the things he speaks
May concern Caesar.

Third Soldier
Let's do so. But he sleeps.

First Soldier
Swoons rather; for so bad a prayer as his
Was never yet for sleep.

Second Soldier
Go we to him.

Third Soldier
Awake, sir, awake; speak to us.

Second Soldier
Hear you, sir?

First Soldier
The hand of death hath raught him.

Drums afar off

Hark! the drums
Demurely wake the sleepers. Let us bear him
To the court of guard; he is of note: our hour
Is fully out.

Third Soldier
Come on, then;
He may recover yet.

Exeunt with the body

SCENE X. Between the two camps.

Enter MARK ANTONY and SCARUS, with their Army

MARK ANTONY
Their preparation is to-day by sea;
We please them not by land.

SCARUS
For both, my lord.

MARK ANTONY
I would they'ld fight i' the fire or i' the air;
We'ld fight there too. But this it is; our foot
Upon the hills adjoining to the city
Shall stay with us: order for sea is given;
They have put forth the haven
Where their appointment we may best discover,
And look on their endeavour.

Exeunt

SCENE XI. Another part of the same.

Enter OCTAVIUS CAESAR, and his Army

OCTAVIUS CAESAR
But being charged, we will be still by land,
Which, as I take't, we shall; for his best force
Is forth to man his galleys. To the vales,
And hold our best advantage.

Exeunt

SCENE XII. Another part of the same.

Enter MARK ANTONY and SCARUS

MARK ANTONY
Yet they are not join'd: where yond pine
does stand,
I shall discover all: I'll bring thee word
Straight, how 'tis like to go.

Exit

SCARUS
Swallows have built
In Cleopatra's sails their nests: the augurers
Say they know not, they cannot tell; look grimly,
And dare not speak their knowledge. Antony
Is valiant, and dejected; and, by starts,
His fretted fortunes give him hope, and fear,
Of what he has, and has not.

Alarum afar off, as at a sea-fight

Re-enter MARK ANTONY

MARK ANTONY
All is lost;
This foul Egyptian hath betrayed me:
My fleet hath yielded to the foe; and yonder
They cast their caps up and carouse together
Like friends long lost. Triple-turn'd whore!
'tis thou
Hast sold me to this novice; and my heart
Makes only wars on thee. Bid them all fly;
For when I am revenged upon my charm,
I have done all. Bid them all fly; begone.

Exit SCARUS

O sun, thy uprise shall I see no more:
Fortune and Antony part here; even here
Do we shake hands. All come to this? The hearts
That spaniel'd me at heels, to whom I gave
Their wishes, do discandy, melt their sweets
On blossoming Caesar; and this pine is bark'd,
That overtopp'd them all. Betray'd I am:
O this false soul of Egypt! this grave charm,--
Whose eye beck'd forth my wars, and call'd them
home;
Whose bosom was my crownet, my chief end,--
Like a right gipsy, hath, at fast and loose,
Beguiled me to the very heart of loss.
What, Eros, Eros!

Enter CLEOPATRA

Ah, thou spell! Avaunt!

CLEOPATRA
Why is my lord enraged against his love?

MARK ANTONY
Vanish, or I shall give thee thy deserving,
And blemish Caesar's triumph. Let him take thee,
And hoist thee up to the shouting plebeians:
Follow his chariot, like the greatest spot
Of all thy sex; most monster-like, be shown
For poor'st diminutives, for doits; and let
Patient Octavia plough thy visage up
With her prepared nails.

Exit CLEOPATRA

'Tis well thou'rt gone,
If it be well to live; but better 'twere
Thou fell'st into my fury, for one death
Might have prevented many. Eros, ho!

The shirt of Nessus is upon me: teach me,
Alcides, thou mine ancestor, thy rage:
Let me lodge Lichas on the horns o' the moon;
And with those hands, that grasp'd the heaviest club,
Subdue my worthiest self. The witch shall die:
To the young Roman boy she hath sold me, and I fall
Under this plot; she dies for't. Eros, ho!

Exit

SCENE XIII. Alexandria. Cleopatra's palace.

Enter CLEOPATRA, CHARMIAN, IRAS, and MARDIAN

CLEOPATRA
Help me, my women! O, he is more mad
Than Telamon for his shield; the boar of Thessaly
Was never so emboss'd.

CHARMIAN
To the monument!
There lock yourself, and send him word you are dead.
The soul and body rive not more in parting
Than greatness going off.

CLEOPATRA
To the monument!
Mardian, go tell him I have slain myself;
Say, that the last I spoke was 'Antony,'
And word it, prithee, piteously: hence, Mardian,
And bring me how he takes my death.
To the monument!

Exeunt

SCENE XIV. The same. Another room.

Enter MARK ANTONY and EROS

MARK ANTONY
Eros, thou yet behold'st me?

EROS
Ay, noble lord.

MARK ANTONY
Sometimes we see a cloud that's dragonish;
A vapour sometime like a bear or lion,
A tower'd citadel, a pendent rock,
A forked mountain, or blue promontory
With trees upon't, that nod unto the world,
And mock our eyes with air: thou hast seen
these signs;
They are black vesper's pageants.

EROS
Ay, my lord,

MARK ANTONY
That which is now a horse, even with a thought
The rack dislimns, and makes it indistinct,
As water is in water.

EROS
It does, my lord.

MARK ANTONY
My good knave Eros, now thy captain is
Even such a body: here I am Antony:
Yet cannot hold this visible shape, my knave.
I made these wars for Egypt: and the queen,--
Whose heart I thought I had, for she had mine;
Which whilst it was mine had annex'd unto't

A million more, now lost,--she, Eros, has
Pack'd cards with Caesar, and false-play'd my glory
Unto an enemy's triumph.
Nay, weep not, gentle Eros; there is left us
Ourselves to end ourselves.

Enter MARDIAN

O! thy vile lady!
She has robb'd me of my sword.

MARDIAN
No, Antony;
My mistress loved thee, and her fortunes mingled
With thine entirely.

MARK ANTONY
Hence, saucy eunuch; peace!
She hath betray'd me and shall die the death.

MARDIAN
Death of one person can be paid but once,
And that she has discharged: what thou wouldst do
Is done unto thy hand: the last she spake
Was 'Antony! most noble Antony!'
Then in the midst a tearing groan did break
The name of Antony; it was divided
Between her heart and lips: she render'd life,
Thy name so buried in her.

MARK ANTONY
Dead, then?

MARDIAN
Dead.

MARK ANTONY
Unarm, Eros; the long day's task is done,
And we must sleep.

To MARDIAN

That thou depart'st hence safe,
Does pay thy labour richly; go.

Exit MARDIAN

Off, pluck off:
The seven-fold shield of Ajax cannot keep
The battery from my heart. O, cleave, my sides!
Heart, once be stronger than thy continent,
Crack thy frail case! Apace, Eros, apace.
No more a soldier: bruised pieces, go;
You have been nobly borne. From me awhile.

Exit EROS

I will o'ertake thee, Cleopatra, and
Weep for my pardon. So it must be, for now
All length is torture: since the torch is out,
Lie down, and stray no farther: now all labour
Mars what it does; yea, very force entangles
Itself with strength: seal then, and all is done.
Eros!--I come, my queen:--Eros!--Stay for me:
Where souls do couch on flowers, we'll hand in hand,
And with our sprightly port make the ghosts gaze:
Dido and her AEneas shall want troops,
And all the haunt be ours. Come, Eros, Eros!

Re-enter EROS

EROS
What would my lord?

MARK ANTONY
Since Cleopatra died,
I have lived in such dishonour, that the gods
Detest my baseness. I, that with my sword

Quarter'd the world, and o'er green Neptune's back
With ships made cities, condemn myself to lack
The courage of a woman; less noble mind
Than she which by her death our Caesar tells
'I am conqueror of myself.' Thou art sworn, Eros,
That, when the exigent should come, which now
Is come indeed, when I should see behind me
The inevitable prosecution of
Disgrace and horror, that, on my command,
Thou then wouldst kill me: do't; the time is come:
Thou strikest not me, 'tis Caesar thou defeat'st.
Put colour in thy cheek.

EROS
The gods withhold me!
Shall I do that which all the Parthian darts,
Though enemy, lost aim, and could not?

MARK ANTONY
Eros,
Wouldst thou be window'd in great Rome and see
Thy master thus with pleach'd arms, bending down
His corrigible neck, his face subdued
To penetrative shame, whilst the wheel'd seat
Of fortunate Caesar, drawn before him, branded
His baseness that ensued?

EROS
I would not see't.

MARK ANTONY
Come, then; for with a wound I must be cured.
Draw that thy honest sword, which thou hast worn
Most useful for thy country.

EROS
O, sir, pardon me!

MARK ANTONY

When I did make thee free, sworest thou not then
To do this when I bade thee? Do it at once;
Or thy precedent services are all
But accidents unpurposed. Draw, and come.

EROS
Turn from me, then, that noble countenance,
Wherein the worship of the whole world lies.

MARK ANTONY
Lo thee!

Turning from him

EROS
My sword is drawn.

MARK ANTONY
Then let it do at once
The thing why thou hast drawn it.

EROS
My dear master,
My captain, and my emperor, let me say,
Before I strike this bloody stroke, farewell.

MARK ANTONY
'Tis said, man; and farewell.

EROS
Farewell, great chief. Shall I strike now?

MARK ANTONY
Now, Eros.

EROS
Why, there then: thus I do escape the sorrow
Of Antony's death.

Kills himself

MARK ANTONY
Thrice-nobler than myself!
Thou teachest me, O valiant Eros, what
I should, and thou couldst not. My queen and Eros
Have by their brave instruction got upon me
A nobleness in record: but I will be
A bridegroom in my death, and run into't
As to a lover's bed. Come, then; and, Eros,
Thy master dies thy scholar: to do thus

Falling on his sword

I learn'd of thee. How! not dead? not dead?
The guard, ho! O, dispatch me!

Enter DERCETAS and Guard

First Guard
What's the noise?

MARK ANTONY
I have done my work in, friends: O, make an end
Of what I have begun.

Second Guard
The star is fall'n.

First Guard
And time is at his period.

All
Alas, and woe!

MARK ANTONY
Let him that loves me strike me dead.

First Guard

Not I.

Second Guard
Nor I.

Third Guard
Nor any one.

Exeunt Guard

DERCETAS
Thy death and fortunes bid thy followers fly.
This sword but shown to Caesar, with this tidings,
Shall enter me with him.

Enter DIOMEDES

DIOMEDES
Where's Antony?

DERCETAS
There, Diomed there.

DIOMEDES
Lives he?
Wilt thou not answer, man?

Exit DERCETAS

MARK ANTONY
Art thou there, Diomed? Draw thy sword, and give me
Sufficing strokes for death.

DIOMEDES
Most absolute lord,
My mistress Cleopatra sent me to thee.

MARK ANTONY
When did she send thee?

DIOMEDES
Now, my lord.

MARK ANTONY
Where is she?

DIOMEDES
Lock'd in her monument. She had a prophesying fear
Of what hath come to pass: for when she saw--
Which never shall be found--you did suspect
She had disposed with Caesar, and that your rage
Would not be purged, she sent you word she was
dead;
But, fearing since how it might work, hath sent
Me to proclaim the truth; and I am come,
I dread, too late.

MARK ANTONY
Too late, good Diomed: call my guard, I prithee.

DIOMEDES
What, ho, the emperor's guard! The guard, what, ho!
Come, your lord calls!

Enter four or five of the Guard of MARK ANTONY

MARK ANTONY
Bear me, good friends, where Cleopatra bides;
'Tis the last service that I shall command you.

First Guard
Woe, woe are we, sir, you may not live to wear
All your true followers out.

All
Most heavy day!

MARK ANTONY
Nay, good my fellows, do not please sharp fate
To grace it with your sorrows: bid that welcome
Which comes to punish us, and we punish it
Seeming to bear it lightly. Take me up:
I have led you oft: carry me now, good friends,
And have my thanks for all.

Exeunt, bearing MARK ANTONY

SCENE XV. The same. A monument.

Enter CLEOPATRA and her maids aloft, with
CHARMIAN and IRAS

CLEOPATRA
O Charmian, I will never go from hence.

CHARMIAN
Be comforted, dear madam.

CLEOPATRA
No, I will not:
All strange and terrible events are welcome,
But comforts we despise; our size of sorrow,
Proportion'd to our cause, must be as great
As that which makes it.

Enter, below, DIOMEDES

How now! is he dead?

DIOMEDES
His death's upon him, but not dead.
Look out o' the other side your monument;
His guard have brought him thither.

Enter, below, MARK ANTONY, borne by the Guard

CLEOPATRA
O sun,
Burn the great sphere thou movest in!
darkling stand
The varying shore o' the world. O Antony,
Antony, Antony! Help, Charmian, help, Iras, help;
Help, friends below; let's draw him hither.

MARK ANTONY
Peace!
Not Caesar's valour hath o'erthrown Antony,
But Antony's hath triumph'd on itself.

CLEOPATRA
So it should be, that none but Antony
Should conquer Antony; but woe 'tis so!

MARK ANTONY
I am dying, Egypt, dying; only
I here importune death awhile, until
Of many thousand kisses the poor last
I lay up thy lips.

CLEOPATRA
I dare not, dear,--
Dear my lord, pardon,--I dare not,
Lest I be taken: not the imperious show
Of the full-fortuned Caesar ever shall
Be brooch'd with me; if knife, drugs,
serpents, have
Edge, sting, or operation, I am safe:
Your wife Octavia, with her modest eyes
And still conclusion, shall acquire no honour
Demuring upon me. But come, come, Antony,--
Help me, my women,--we must draw thee up:
Assist, good friends.

MARK ANTONY
O, quick, or I am gone.

CLEOPATRA
Here's sport indeed! How heavy weighs my lord!
Our strength is all gone into heaviness,
That makes the weight: had I great Juno's power,
The strong-wing'd Mercury should fetch thee up,
And set thee by Jove's side. Yet come a little,--
Wishes were ever fools,--O, come, come, come;

They heave MARK ANTONY aloft to CLEOPATRA

And welcome, welcome! die where thou hast lived:
Quicken with kissing: had my lips that power,
Thus would I wear them out.

All
A heavy sight!

MARK ANTONY
I am dying, Egypt, dying:
Give me some wine, and let me speak a little.

CLEOPATRA
No, let me speak; and let me rail so high,
That the false housewife Fortune break her wheel,
Provoked by my offence.

MARK ANTONY
One word, sweet queen:
Of Caesar seek your honour, with your safety. O!

CLEOPATRA
They do not go together.

MARK ANTONY
Gentle, hear me:
None about Caesar trust but Proculeius.

CLEOPATRA
My resolution and my hands I'll trust;
None about Caesar.

MARK ANTONY
The miserable change now at my end
Lament nor sorrow at; but please your thoughts
In feeding them with those my former fortunes
Wherein I lived, the greatest prince o' the world,

The noblest; and do now not basely die,
Not cowardly put off my helmet to
My countryman,--a Roman by a Roman
Valiantly vanquish'd. Now my spirit is going;
I can no more.

CLEOPATRA
Noblest of men, woo't die?
Hast thou no care of me? shall I abide
In this dull world, which in thy absence is
No better than a sty? O, see, my women,

MARK ANTONY dies

The crown o' the earth doth melt. My lord!
O, wither'd is the garland of the war,
The soldier's pole is fall'n: young boys and girls
Are level now with men; the odds is gone,
And there is nothing left remarkable
Beneath the visiting moon.

Faints

CHARMIAN
O, quietness, lady!

IRAS
She is dead too, our sovereign.

CHARMIAN
Lady!

IRAS
Madam!

CHARMIAN
O madam, madam, madam!

IRAS
Royal Egypt, Empress!

CHARMIAN
Peace, peace, Iras!

CLEOPATRA
No more, but e'en a woman, and commanded
By such poor passion as the maid that milks
And does the meanest chares. It were for me
To throw my sceptre at the injurious gods;
To tell them that this world did equal theirs
Till they had stol'n our jewel. All's but naught;
Patience is scottish, and impatience does
Become a dog that's mad: then is it sin
To rush into the secret house of death,
Ere death dare come to us? How do you, women?
What, what! good cheer! Why, how now, Charmian!
My noble girls! Ah, women, women, look,
Our lamp is spent, it's out! Good sirs, take heart:
We'll bury him; and then, what's brave,
what's noble,
Let's do it after the high Roman fashion,
And make death proud to take us. Come, away:
This case of that huge spirit now is cold:
Ah, women, women! come; we have no friend
But resolution, and the briefest end.

Exeunt; those above bearing off MARK ANTONY's body

ACT V

SCENE I. Alexandria. OCTAVIUS CAESAR's camp.

Enter OCTAVIUS CAESAR, AGRIPPA, DOLABELLA,
MECAENAS, GALLUS, PROCULEIUS, and others, his
council of war

OCTAVIUS CAESAR
Go to him, Dolabella, bid him yield;
Being so frustrate, tell him he mocks
The pauses that he makes.

DOLABELLA
Caesar, I shall.

Exit

Enter DERCETAS, with the sword of MARK ANTONY

OCTAVIUS CAESAR
Wherefore is that? and what art thou that darest
Appear thus to us?

DERCETAS
I am call'd Dercetas;
Mark Antony I served, who best was worthy
Best to be served: whilst he stood up and spoke,
He was my master; and I wore my life
To spend upon his haters. If thou please
To take me to thee, as I was to him
I'll be to Caesar; if thou pleasest not,
I yield thee up my life.

OCTAVIUS CAESAR
What is't thou say'st?

DERCETAS
I say, O Caesar, Antony is dead.

OCTAVIUS CAESAR
The breaking of so great a thing should make
A greater crack: the round world
Should have shook lions into civil streets,
And citizens to their dens: the death of Antony
Is not a single doom; in the name lay
A moiety of the world.

DERCETAS
He is dead, Caesar:
Not by a public minister of justice,
Nor by a hired knife; but that self hand,
Which writ his honour in the acts it did,
Hath, with the courage which the heart did lend it,
Splitted the heart. This is his sword;
I robb'd his wound of it; behold it stain'd
With his most noble blood.

OCTAVIUS CAESAR
Look you sad, friends?
The gods rebuke me, but it is tidings
To wash the eyes of kings.

AGRIPPA
And strange it is,
That nature must compel us to lament
Our most persisted deeds.

MECAENAS
His taints and honours
Waged equal with him.

AGRIPPA
A rarer spirit never
Did steer humanity: but you, gods, will give us
Some faults to make us men. Caesar is touch'd.

MECAENAS
When such a spacious mirror's set before him,
He needs must see himself.

OCTAVIUS CAESAR
O Antony!
I have follow'd thee to this; but we do lance
Diseases in our bodies: I must perforce
Have shown to thee such a declining day,
Or look on thine; we could not stall together
In the whole world: but yet let me lament,
With tears as sovereign as the blood of hearts,
That thou, my brother, my competitor
In top of all design, my mate in empire,
Friend and companion in the front of war,
The arm of mine own body, and the heart
Where mine his thoughts did kindle,--that our stars,
Unreconciliable, should divide
Our equalness to this. Hear me, good friends--
But I will tell you at some meeter season:

Enter an Egyptian

The business of this man looks out of him;
We'll hear him what he says. Whence are you?

Egyptian
A poor Egyptian yet. The queen my mistress,
Confined in all she has, her monument,
Of thy intents desires instruction,
That she preparedly may frame herself
To the way she's forced to.

OCTAVIUS CAESAR
Bid her have good heart:
She soon shall know of us, by some of ours,
How honourable and how kindly we
Determine for her; for Caesar cannot live

To be ungentle.

Egyptian
So the gods preserve thee!

Exit

OCTAVIUS CAESAR
Come hither, Proculeius. Go and say,
We purpose her no shame: give her what comforts
The quality of her passion shall require,
Lest, in her greatness, by some mortal stroke
She do defeat us; for her life in Rome
Would be eternal in our triumph: go,
And with your speediest bring us what she says,
And how you find of her.

PROCULEIUS
Caesar, I shall.

Exit

OCTAVIUS CAESAR
Gallus, go you along.

Exit GALLUS

Where's Dolabella,
To second Proculeius?

All
Dolabella!

OCTAVIUS CAESAR
Let him alone, for I remember now
How he's employ'd: he shall in time be ready.
Go with me to my tent; where you shall see
How hardly I was drawn into this war;
How calm and gentle I proceeded still

In all my writings: go with me, and see
What I can show in this.

Exeunt

SCENE II. Alexandria. A room in the monument.

Enter CLEOPATRA, CHARMIAN, and IRAS

CLEOPATRA
My desolation does begin to make
A better life. 'Tis paltry to be Caesar;
Not being Fortune, he's but Fortune's knave,
A minister of her will: and it is great
To do that thing that ends all other deeds;
Which shackles accidents and bolts up change;
Which sleeps, and never palates more the dug,
The beggar's nurse and Caesar's.

Enter, to the gates of the monument, PROCULEIUS,
GALLUS and Soldiers

PROCULEIUS
Caesar sends greeting to the Queen of Egypt;
And bids thee study on what fair demands
Thou mean'st to have him grant thee.

CLEOPATRA
What's thy name?

PROCULEIUS
My name is Proculeius.

CLEOPATRA
Antony
Did tell me of you, bade me trust you; but
I do not greatly care to be deceived,
That have no use for trusting. If your master
Would have a queen his beggar, you must tell him,
That majesty, to keep decorum, must
No less beg than a kingdom: if he please
To give me conquer'd Egypt for my son,
He gives me so much of mine own, as I

Will kneel to him with thanks.

PROCULEIUS
Be of good cheer;
You're fall'n into a princely hand, fear nothing:
Make your full reference freely to my lord,
Who is so full of grace, that it flows over
On all that need: let me report to him
Your sweet dependency; and you shall find
A conqueror that will pray in aid for kindness,
Where he for grace is kneel'd to.

CLEOPATRA
Pray you, tell him
I am his fortune's vassal, and I send him
The greatness he has got. I hourly learn
A doctrine of obedience; and would gladly
Look him i' the face.

PROCULEIUS
This I'll report, dear lady.
Have comfort, for I know your plight is pitied
Of him that caused it.

GALLUS
You see how easily she may be surprised:

Here PROCULEIUS and two of the Guard ascend the
monument by a ladder placed against a window, and,
having descended, come behind CLEOPATRA. Some of
the Guard unbar and open the gates

To PROCULEIUS and the Guard

Guard her till Caesar come.

Exit

IRAS
Royal queen!

CHARMIAN
O Cleopatra! thou art taken, queen:

CLEOPATRA
Quick, quick, good hands.

Drawing a dagger

PROCULEIUS
Hold, worthy lady, hold:

Seizes and disarms her

Do not yourself such wrong, who are in this
Relieved, but not betray'd.

CLEOPATRA
What, of death too,
That rids our dogs of languish?

PROCULEIUS
Cleopatra,
Do not abuse my master's bounty by
The undoing of yourself: let the world see
His nobleness well acted, which your death
Will never let come forth.

CLEOPATRA
Where art thou, death?
Come hither, come! come, come, and take a queen
Worthy many babes and beggars!

PROCULEIUS
O, temperance, lady!

CLEOPATRA
Sir, I will eat no meat, I'll not drink, sir;
If idle talk will once be necessary,
I'll not sleep neither: this mortal house I'll ruin,
Do Caesar what he can. Know, sir, that I
Will not wait pinion'd at your master's court;
Nor once be chastised with the sober eye
Of dull Octavia. Shall they hoist me up
And show me to the shouting varletry
Of censuring Rome? Rather a ditch in Egypt
Be gentle grave unto me! rather on Nilus' mud
Lay me stark naked, and let the water-flies
Blow me into abhorring! rather make
My country's high pyramides my gibbet,
And hang me up in chains!

PROCULEIUS
You do extend
These thoughts of horror further than you shall
Find cause in Caesar.

Enter DOLABELLA

DOLABELLA
Proculeius,
What thou hast done thy master Caesar knows,
And he hath sent for thee: for the queen,
I'll take her to my guard.

PROCULEIUS
So, Dolabella,
It shall content me best: be gentle to her.

To CLEOPATRA

To Caesar I will speak what you shall please,
If you'll employ me to him.

CLEOPATRA
Say, I would die.

Exeunt PROCULEIUS and Soldiers

DOLABELLA
Most noble empress, you have heard of me?

CLEOPATRA
I cannot tell.

DOLABELLA
Assuredly you know me.

CLEOPATRA
No matter, sir, what I have heard or known.
You laugh when boys or women tell their dreams;
Is't not your trick?

DOLABELLA
I understand not, madam.

CLEOPATRA
I dream'd there was an Emperor Antony:
O, such another sleep, that I might see
But such another man!

DOLABELLA
If it might please ye,--

CLEOPATRA
His face was as the heavens; and therein stuck
A sun and moon, which kept their course,
and lighted
The little O, the earth.

DOLABELLA
Most sovereign creature,--

CLEOPATRA
His legs bestrid the ocean: his rear'd arm
Crested the world: his voice was propertied
As all the tuned spheres, and that to friends;
But when he meant to quail and shake the orb,
He was as rattling thunder. For his bounty,
There was no winter in't; an autumn 'twas
That grew the more by reaping: his delights
Were dolphin-like; they show'd his back above
The element they lived in: in his livery
Walk'd crowns and crownets; realms and islands were
As plates dropp'd from his pocket.

DOLABELLA
Cleopatra!

CLEOPATRA
Think you there was, or might be, such a man
As this I dream'd of?

DOLABELLA
Gentle madam, no.

CLEOPATRA
You lie, up to the hearing of the gods.
But, if there be, or ever were, one such,
It's past the size of dreaming: nature wants stuff
To vie strange forms with fancy; yet, to imagine
And Antony, were nature's piece 'gainst fancy,
Condemning shadows quite.

DOLABELLA
Hear me, good madam.
Your loss is as yourself, great; and you bear it
As answering to the weight: would I might never
O'ertake pursued success, but I do feel,
By the rebound of yours, a grief that smites
My very heart at root.

CLEOPATRA
I thank you, sir,
Know you what Caesar means to do with me?

DOLABELLA
I am loath to tell you what I would you knew.

CLEOPATRA
Nay, pray you, sir,--

DOLABELLA
Though he be honourable,--

CLEOPATRA
He'll lead me, then, in triumph?

DOLABELLA
Madam, he will; I know't.

Flourish, and shout within, 'Make way there: Octavius
Caesar!'

Enter OCTAVIUS CAESAR, GALLUS, PROCULEIUS,
MECAENAS, SELEUCUS, and others of his Train

OCTAVIUS CAESAR
Which is the Queen of Egypt?

DOLABELLA
It is the emperor, madam.

CLEOPATRA kneels

OCTAVIUS CAESAR
Arise, you shall not kneel:
I pray you, rise; rise, Egypt.

CLEOPATRA
Sir, the gods

Will have it thus; my master and my lord
I must obey.

OCTAVIUS CAESAR
Take to you no hard thoughts:
The record of what injuries you did us,
Though written in our flesh, we shall remember
As things but done by chance.

CLEOPATRA
Sole sir o' the world,
I cannot project mine own cause so well
To make it clear; but do confess I have
Been laden with like frailties which before
Have often shamed our sex.

OCTAVIUS CAESAR
Cleopatra, know,
We will extenuate rather than enforce:
If you apply yourself to our intents,
Which towards you are most gentle, you shall find
A benefit in this change; but if you seek
To lay on me a cruelty, by taking
Antony's course, you shall bereave yourself
Of my good purposes, and put your children
To that destruction which I'll guard them from,
If thereon you rely. I'll take my leave.

CLEOPATRA
And may, through all the world: 'tis yours; and we,
Your scutcheons and your signs of conquest, shall
Hang in what place you please. Here, my good lord.

OCTAVIUS CAESAR
You shall advise me in all for Cleopatra.

CLEOPATRA
This is the brief of money, plate, and jewels,
I am possess'd of: 'tis exactly valued;

Not petty things admitted. Where's Seleucus?

SELEUCUS
Here, madam.

CLEOPATRA
This is my treasurer: let him speak, my lord,
Upon his peril, that I have reserved
To myself nothing. Speak the truth, Seleucus.

SELEUCUS
Madam,
I had rather seal my lips, than, to my peril,
Speak that which is not.

CLEOPATRA
What have I kept back?

SELEUCUS
Enough to purchase what you have made known.

OCTAVIUS CAESAR
Nay, blush not, Cleopatra; I approve
Your wisdom in the deed.

CLEOPATRA
See, Caesar! O, behold,
How pomp is follow'd! mine will now be yours;
And, should we shift estates, yours would be mine.
The ingratitude of this Seleucus does
Even make me wild: O slave, of no more trust
Than love that's hired! What, goest thou back? thou
shalt
Go back, I warrant thee; but I'll catch thine eyes,
Though they had wings: slave, soulless villain, dog!
O rarely base!

OCTAVIUS CAESAR
Good queen, let us entreat you.

CLEOPATRA
O Caesar, what a wounding shame is this,
That thou, vouchsafing here to visit me,
Doing the honour of thy lordliness
To one so meek, that mine own servant should
Parcel the sum of my disgraces by
Addition of his envy! Say, good Caesar,
That I some lady trifles have reserved,
Immoment toys, things of such dignity
As we greet modern friends withal; and say,
Some nobler token I have kept apart
For Livia and Octavia, to induce
Their mediation; must I be unfolded
With one that I have bred? The gods! it smites me
Beneath the fall I have.

To SELEUCUS

Prithee, go hence;
Or I shall show the cinders of my spirits
Through the ashes of my chance: wert thou a man,
Thou wouldst have mercy on me.

OCTAVIUS CAESAR
Forbear, Seleucus.

Exit SELEUCUS

CLEOPATRA
Be it known, that we, the greatest, are misthought
For things that others do; and, when we fall,
We answer others' merits in our name,
Are therefore to be pitied.

OCTAVIUS CAESAR
Cleopatra,
Not what you have reserved, nor what acknowledged,
Put we i' the roll of conquest: still be't yours,

Bestow it at your pleasure; and believe,
Caesar's no merchant, to make prize with you
Of things that merchants sold. Therefore be cheer'd;
Make not your thoughts your prisons: no, dear queen;
For we intend so to dispose you as
Yourself shall give us counsel. Feed, and sleep:
Our care and pity is so much upon you,
That we remain your friend; and so, adieu.

CLEOPATRA
My master, and my lord!

OCTAVIUS CAESAR
Not so. Adieu.

Flourish. Exeunt OCTAVIUS CAESAR and his train

CLEOPATRA
He words me, girls, he words me, that I should not
Be noble to myself: but, hark thee, Charmian.

Whispers CHARMIAN

IRAS
Finish, good lady; the bright day is done,
And we are for the dark.

CLEOPATRA
Hie thee again:
I have spoke already, and it is provided;
Go put it to the haste.

CHARMIAN
Madam, I will.

Re-enter DOLABELLA

DOLABELLA
Where is the queen?

CHARMIAN
Behold, sir.

Exit

CLEOPATRA
Dolabella!

DOLABELLA
Madam, as thereto sworn by your command,
Which my love makes religion to obey,
I tell you this: Caesar through Syria
Intends his journey; and within three days
You with your children will he send before:
Make your best use of this: I have perform'd
Your pleasure and my promise.

CLEOPATRA
Dolabella,
I shall remain your debtor.

DOLABELLA
I your servant,
Adieu, good queen; I must attend on Caesar.

CLEOPATRA
Farewell, and thanks.

Exit DOLABELLA

Now, Iras, what think'st thou?
Thou, an Egyptian puppet, shalt be shown
In Rome, as well as I mechanic slaves
With greasy aprons, rules, and hammers, shall
Uplift us to the view; in their thick breaths,
Rank of gross diet, shall be enclouded,
And forced to drink their vapour.

IRAS
The gods forbid!

CLEOPATRA
Nay, 'tis most certain, Iras: saucy lictors
Will catch at us, like strumpets; and scald rhymers
Ballad us out o' tune: the quick comedians
Extemporally will stage us, and present
Our Alexandrian revels; Antony
Shall be brought drunken forth, and I shall see
Some squeaking Cleopatra boy my greatness
I' the posture of a whore.

IRAS
O the good gods!

CLEOPATRA
Nay, that's certain.

IRAS
I'll never see 't; for, I am sure, my nails
Are stronger than mine eyes.

CLEOPATRA
Why, that's the way
To fool their preparation, and to conquer
Their most absurd intents.

Re-enter CHARMIAN

Now, Charmian!
Show me, my women, like a queen: go fetch
My best attires: I am again for Cydnus,
To meet Mark Antony: sirrah Iras, go.
Now, noble Charmian, we'll dispatch indeed;
And, when thou hast done this chare, I'll give thee leave
To play till doomsday. Bring our crown and all.
Wherefore's this noise?

Exit IRAS. A noise within

Enter a Guardsman

Guard
Here is a rural fellow
That will not be denied your highness presence:
He brings you figs.

CLEOPATRA
Let him come in.

Exit Guardsman

What poor an instrument
May do a noble deed! he brings me liberty.
My resolution's placed, and I have nothing
Of woman in me: now from head to foot
I am marble-constant; now the fleeting moon
No planet is of mine.

Re-enter Guardsman, with Clown bringing in a basket

Guard
This is the man.

CLEOPATRA
Avoid, and leave him.

Exit Guardsman

Hast thou the pretty worm of Nilus there,
That kills and pains not?

Clown
Truly, I have him: but I would not be the party
that should desire you to touch him, for his biting
is immortal; those that do die of it do seldom or

never recover.

CLEOPATRA
Rememberest thou any that have died on't?

Clown
Very many, men and women too. I heard of one of
them no longer than yesterday: a very honest woman,
but something given to lie; as a woman should not
do, but in the way of honesty: how she died of the
biting of it, what pain she felt: truly, she makes
a very good report o' the worm; but he that will
believe all that they say, shall never be saved by
half that they do: but this is most fallible, the
worm's an odd worm.

CLEOPATRA
Get thee hence; farewell.

Clown
I wish you all joy of the worm.

Setting down his basket

CLEOPATRA
Farewell.

Clown
You must think this, look you, that the worm will
do his kind.

CLEOPATRA
Ay, ay; farewell.

Clown
Look you, the worm is not to be trusted but in the
keeping of wise people; for, indeed, there is no
goodness in worm.

CLEOPATRA
Take thou no care; it shall be heeded.

Clown
Very good. Give it nothing, I pray you, for it is
not worth the feeding.

CLEOPATRA
Will it eat me?

Clown
You must not think I am so simple but I know the
devil himself will not eat a woman: I know that a
woman is a dish for the gods, if the devil dress her
not. But, truly, these same whoreson devils do the
gods great harm in their women; for in every ten
that they make, the devils mar five.

CLEOPATRA
Well, get thee gone; farewell.

Clown
Yes, forsooth: I wish you joy o' the worm.

Exit

Re-enter IRAS with a robe, crown, & c

CLEOPATRA
Give me my robe, put on my crown; I have
Immortal longings in me: now no more
The juice of Egypt's grape shall moist this lip:
Yare, yare, good Iras; quick. Methinks I hear
Antony call; I see him rouse himself
To praise my noble act; I hear him mock
The luck of Caesar, which the gods give men
To excuse their after wrath: husband, I come:
Now to that name my courage prove my title!
I am fire and air; my other elements

I give to baser life. So; have you done?
Come then, and take the last warmth of my lips.
Farewell, kind Charmian; Iras, long farewell.

Kisses them. IRAS falls and dies

Have I the aspic in my lips? Dost fall?
If thou and nature can so gently part,
The stroke of death is as a lover's pinch,
Which hurts, and is desired. Dost thou lie still?
If thus thou vanishest, thou tell'st the world
It is not worth leave-taking.

CHARMIAN
Dissolve, thick cloud, and rain; that I may say,
The gods themselves do weep!

CLEOPATRA
This proves me base:
If she first meet the curled Antony,
He'll make demand of her, and spend that kiss
Which is my heaven to have. Come, thou
mortal wretch,

To an asp, which she applies to her breast

With thy sharp teeth this knot intrinsicate
Of life at once untie: poor venomous fool
Be angry, and dispatch. O, couldst thou speak,
That I might hear thee call great Caesar ass
Unpolicied!

CHARMIAN
O eastern star!

CLEOPATRA
Peace, peace!
Dost thou not see my baby at my breast,
That sucks the nurse asleep?

CHARMIAN
O, break! O, break!

CLEOPATRA
As sweet as balm, as soft as air, as gentle,--
O Antony!--Nay, I will take thee too.

Applying another asp to her arm

What should I stay--

Dies

CHARMIAN
In this vile world? So, fare thee well.
Now boast thee, death, in thy possession lies
A lass unparallel'd. Downy windows, close;
And golden Phoebus never be beheld
Of eyes again so royal! Your crown's awry;
I'll mend it, and then play.

Enter the Guard, rushing in

First Guard
Where is the queen?

CHARMIAN
Speak softly, wake her not.

First Guard
Caesar hath sent--

CHARMIAN
Too slow a messenger.

Applies an asp

O, come apace, dispatch! I partly feel thee.

First Guard
Approach, ho! All's not well: Caesar's beguiled.

Second Guard
There's Dolabella sent from Caesar; call him.

First Guard
What work is here! Charmian, is this well done?

CHARMIAN
It is well done, and fitting for a princess
Descended of so many royal kings.
Ah, soldier!

Dies

Re-enter DOLABELLA

DOLABELLA
How goes it here?

Second Guard
All dead.

DOLABELLA
Caesar, thy thoughts
Touch their effects in this: thyself art coming
To see perform'd the dreaded act which thou
So sought'st to hinder.

Within 'A way there, a way for Caesar!'

Re-enter OCTAVIUS CAESAR and all his train
marching

DOLABELLA
O sir, you are too sure an augurer;
That you did fear is done.

OCTAVIUS CAESAR
Bravest at the last,
She levell'd at our purposes, and, being royal,
Took her own way. The manner of their deaths?
I do not see them bleed.

DOLABELLA
Who was last with them?

First Guard
A simple countryman, that brought her figs:
This was his basket.

OCTAVIUS CAESAR
Poison'd, then.

First Guard
O Caesar,
This Charmian lived but now; she stood and spake:
I found her trimming up the diadem
On her dead mistress; tremblingly she stood
And on the sudden dropp'd.

OCTAVIUS CAESAR
O noble weakness!
If they had swallow'd poison, 'twould appear
By external swelling: but she looks like sleep,
As she would catch another Antony
In her strong toil of grace.

DOLABELLA
Here, on her breast,
There is a vent of blood and something blown:
The like is on her arm.

First Guard
This is an aspic's trail: and these fig-leaves
Have slime upon them, such as the aspic leaves

Upon the caves of Nile.

OCTAVIUS CAESAR
Most probable
That so she died; for her physician tells me
She hath pursued conclusions infinite
Of easy ways to die. Take up her bed;
And bear her women from the monument:
She shall be buried by her Antony:
No grave upon the earth shall clip in it
A pair so famous. High events as these
Strike those that make them; and their story is
No less in pity than his glory which
Brought them to be lamented. Our army shall
In solemn show attend this funeral;
And then to Rome. Come, Dolabella, see
High order in this great solemnity.

Exeunt

CPSIA information can be obtained at www.ICGtesting.com
Printed in the USA
LVOW07s1625220916

505792LV00001B/252/P